Also by Jerold Panas

The Fundraising Habits of Supremely Successful Boards

Over the course of a storied career, Jerold Panas has worked with literally thousands of boards, from those governing the toniest of prep schools to those spearheading the local Y.

He has counseled floundering groups; he has been the wind beneath the wings of boards whose organizations have soared.

In fact, it's a safe bet that Panas has observed more boards than perhaps anyone in America, all the while helping them to surpass their campaign goals of $100,000 to $100 million.

Funnel every ounce of that experience and wisdom into a single book and what you have is *The Fundraising Habits of Supremely Successful Boards*, the brilliant culmination of what Panas has learned firsthand about boards who excel at the task of resource development.

Anyone who has read *Asking* or any of Panas' other books knows his style – a breezy and irresistible mix of storytelling, exhortation, and inspiration.

Habits follows the same engaging mold, offering a panoply of habits any board would be wise to cultivate. Some are specific, with measurable outcomes. Others are more intangible, with Panas seeking to impart an attitude of success.

In all, there are 25 habits and each is explored in two- and three-page chapters ... and all of them animated by real-life stories only this grandmaster of philanthropy can tell.

In a mere 117 pages, about an hour's read, Jerold Panas has accomplished two feats. He has produced a book that boards will find simultaneously ennobling *and* instructive. And he has relegated to the recycling bin dozens upon dozens of ponderous and inauthentic treatises on the subject of nonprofit boards and fundraising.

MEGA GIFTS

Who Gives Them, Who Gets Them

10 9 8 7 6 5

Printed in the United States of America

This text is printed on acid-free paper.

ISBN: 1-889102-24-5

Emerson & Church, Publishers
15 Brook Street, Medfield, MA 02052
Tel. 508-359-0019
Fax 508-359-2703
www.emersonandchurch.com

Library of Congress Cataloging-in-Publication Data

Panas, Jerold.
  Megagifts : who gives them, who gets them? / Jerold Panas.-- 2nd ed.
  p. cm.
Includes index
  ISBN 1-889102-24-5 (pbk. : alk. paper)
  1. Endowments--United States. 2. Gifts--United States. I. Title:
Mega gifts. II. Title.
  HV41.P34 2005
  361.7'0973--dc22
                                                    2005000858

MEGA GIFTS

Who Gives Them,
Who Gets Them

Second Edition

JEROLD PANAS

Emerson
& Church
PUBLISHERS

OF RELATED INTEREST

**Fund Raising Realities
Every Board Member Must Face**

A 1-Hour Crash Course on Raising
Major Gifts for Nonprofit Organizations

David Lansdowne

If every board member of every nonprofit organization across America read this book, it's no exaggeration to say that millions upon millions of additional dollars would be raised.

How could it be otherwise when, after spending just *one* hour with this gem, board members everywhere would understand virtually everything they need to know about raising major gifts.

David Lansdowne distills the essence of major gifts fundraising, puts it in the context of 47 "realities," and delivers it all in unfailingly clear prose.

Among the *Top Three* bestselling fundraising books of all time.

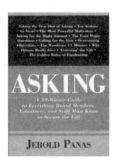

ASKING

A 59-Minute Guide to Everything
Board Members, Volunteers, and Staff
Must Know to Secure the Gift

Jerold Panas

It ranks right up there with public speaking. Nearly all of us fear it. And yet it's critical to the success of our organizations. Asking for money. It makes even the stout-hearted quiver.

But now comes a book, *Asking*, and short of a medical elixir, it's the next best thing for emboldening board members, volunteers, and staff to ask with skill, finesse ... and powerful results.

What *Asking* convincingly shows is that it doesn't take stellar sales skills to be an effective asker. Nearly everyone, regardless of their persuasive ability, can become an effective fundraiser if they follow Panas' step-by-step guidelines.

Emerson & Church, Publishers
www.emersonandchurch.com

"Blessed are the money raisers ...
for in heaven, they shall stand
on the right hand of the martyrs."

– John R. Mott

Dedication

This book is dedicated to the hundreds
of thousands of professionals and volunteers
involved in fundraising for great causes,
toilers all in the vineyards of philanthropy.

CONTENTS

A Personal Note

When I began writing *Mega Gifts*, I wasn't keen on producing another 'how-to' tract on fundraising. There were already a number of them at the library, a few of them quite good.

And I felt strongly that one of my missions in life was to save the world from yet another book on campaign structure. There were already dozens of these, too.

Fortunately, I had a publisher who agreed. "I don't want any of that – and I certainly don't want a rehash of basics," he insisted.

"What makes people give big gifts? Really big gifts. What's their motivation? That's what I want to know. Peel away all the layers and get to the heart of it."

That imperative led me to write the first edition of *Mega Gifts*. What evolved was an extraordinary journey. And a book unlike any other in the field.

I had in-depth interviews with close to 50 men and women who had made gifts of $1 million or more (some had made many gifts at that level).

But I didn't stop there. To corroborate what I learned from these mega givers, I surveyed nearly a thousand fundraisers in the field. I synthesized their thoughts and observations.

Setting the figure at $1 million was arbitrary. On the other hand, there is something singular about it. A six-figure gift is special, but that's taking it to the two or three-yard line. A $1 million gift somehow symbolizes taking it over the goal line.

No one was eager to be interviewed. Mostly, these are very private people. Because they were mostly friends, I had the freedom to probe, question, and explore. No holds barred.

In the updated and revised edition you now hold, I've added a number of new stories, all true. There are more chapters. And many fresh insights. Equally important, I bring 20 additional years of experience to the field. And a great deal more association with mega givers.

As you'll find, consistent themes emerge and merge in the book. For me, that's the most intriguing part. Uncovering aspirations common to this very select group of donors.

I use quotations heavily because they speak

so vividly and pointedly to the issue. Dissecting the donors' words, analyzing the variables point by point, would in some way destroy their essence – the human and intense quality, and the emotional impact of giving.

My wish is that this new edition will challenge you to think smarter, work harder, plan bolder, and commit yourself with fervor and missionary zeal to the needs of your institution.

More than anything, I hope the book provides you with a daring willingness to challenge, to explore, to break through old barriers.

One last word. I realize many of you will be approaching donors who give far less than $1 million. Don't be concerned. This book and its principles are every bit as relevant for $100 donors. I should know, I've approached my share of those, too.

The great French author, Margaurite Duras wrote: "The book doesn't really end. As it closes, it is just a beginning." If *Mega Gifts* does not provide a precise road map, perhaps it does contain helpful directional signs and landmarks. At the least, it will be a beginning.

1

THE INCREDIBLE ODYSSEY

"The Mock Turtle, in a deep hollow tone, said: 'Sit down, and don't speak a word 'til I've finished.' So they sat down and nobody spoke for some minutes. Alice thought to herself, 'I don't see how he can ever finish if he doesn't begin.'"

– Lewis Carroll
Alice in Wonderland

He was wearing a gray suit. He almost always did. Those who knew him best said he had a closet filled with them. Each meticulously hand sewn. Each very expensive. Each three piece.

Moses Annenberg was walking down Wall Street in New York City with his son Walter – a freshman at Peddie, at the time a not too distinguished prep school in New Jersey.

It was scorching that August day in 1925, the

hottest oldtimers could remember. But in spite of the heat, Moses had each button of his vest and each button of his jacket firmly in place.

There was great affection between these two, father and son. Moses would see to it that the young boy would inherit everything. A not inconsiderable sum. As for Walter, he idolized his father, tried to emulate him in every way possible.

As they walked, Moses reached into his pocket. A couple dollars for a derelict. A handful of coins for a man begging on the corner. A dollar in the tin cup of a blind man.

"Just remember," Moses admonished his son, "there but for the grace of God go you and I."

Raised in abject poverty, Moses built a publishing empire that included *The Philadelphia Inquirer* and *Miami Tribune*. But always he believed in what Isaac Asimov called the "genetic sweepstakes."

Some people are endowed with more than others. It's the luck of the draw. Time after time, Moses impressed on his son that the lucky ones had a responsibility to help the less fortunate.

They continued their walk down Wall Street, turned up Worth on their way to Broadway. Another beggar, another handful of coins.

Actually, it wasn't charity for Moses. It was raw, impulsive superstition. He felt some mild sense of compassion, but mostly he thought by helping the less fortunate, he could count on his incredible good luck continuing.

It was his compulsion, his motivating philosophy of life. Give, and it comes back to you. Help the poor and the needy. If you do, you will prosper. It was a seed planted in young Walter's mind.

Even at the time, young Walter Annenberg had a keen sense of pride that made him want the best.

During his high school graduation activities in 1927, the teenage Annenberg donated $17,000 for a new track – the first of countless gifts amounting to over $200 million he would bestow on Peddie School.

He virtually rebuilt the School's campus, including new dormitories, a library, a gymnasium, and a planetarium. It was his way of making it one of the nation's superior prep schools.

When Walter returned to the States after serving, under President Nixon, as Ambassador to the Court of St. James, he promptly established a Child Day Care Center at the Desert Hospital in Palm Springs, California. Its purpose was to provide aid and comfort to abused children.

He became acutely aware of the problem shortly before he left his Embassy post. In a London paper he came across an article about a little girl who had been grossly harmed by her father.

It was unthinkable to Annenberg that a parent could really do such a thing. So he went to the hospital to see for himself and to speak with the child.

It was true. She had been battered, abused, molested. Her whole body was covered with burns from a cigarette. "When I saw what had been done to her," he said. "I felt sick and knew I had to do something to help these children."

Walter Annenberg was one of the great benefactors of this nation. His gift of $150 million for a communications complex at the University of Pennsylvania was at the time the largest single private gift ever given by a living person. He followed that with a gift of $300 million for public education.

Who can be certain of the impetus that motivated this prodigious generosity?

Could it have been recognition and tribute? Hardly likely. He was very private and eschewed identification with his gifts. A great commitment to the plight and concerns of the needy? Probably not. The greatest majority of his gifts were for special programs and the general good of mankind, but not for the oppressed and needy.

Perhaps it was superstition, to guarantee his continued good luck? It is hard to say and probably Walter Annenberg himself couldn't have unlocked the answer to the puzzle.

The rise of Julius Rosenwald's fortunes from meager resources to unimaginable riches is a Horatio Alger story of extraordinary proportions. It is one of the most dramatic in the nation's history.

By sheer accident Rosenwald became a partner and major stockholder in Sears-Roebuck. Pure serendipity. He was at the right place at the right time.

The fact that he quickly bought out his brother-in-law for a pittance in order to take control of the company is another matter.

It was Rosenwald's genius that built the company. His fortune grew from virtually nothing to an estimated $600 million. All this in just seven years. Today that would equate to $300 billion!

He was a strange mixture, Julius Rosenwald. His personal spending habits were extraordinary. He thought nothing, for instance, of building tennis courts on the grounds of his baronial home. He flatly refused to buy tennis balls, however, opting to use those of his opponent.

Odd as his spending habits were, he loved giving money away. It was his passion.

In Rosenwald's case, the recipients were the poor. His special concern was for the deplorable condition of young blacks, particularly in the South. To help remedy their situation, he set about building what became known as "Rosenwald Schools."

All told, there were over 5000 schools, shops, and housing units scattered throughout the Southern states. A hundred YMCAs were built for blacks.

There was scholarship assistance and fellowships. All for blacks and all segregated. That was the pattern of the time.

What was unusual about Rosenwald's giving was that it followed an unpopular course at the time.

It was totally unlike the other great Jewish philanthropists – Schiff, Warburg, Kahn – who gave to more conventional institutions: the museums, the medical centers, the "proper and approved" institutions.

Some wags claim Rosenwald was mindful of the fact that his growing fortunes were related directly to the ability of blacks to buy goods from those exciting, new Sears catalogues. As their ability to pay for merchandise grew, Rosenwald prospered.

What truly motivated his giving? A selfishness? An over-expanded ego? Or a strong commitment to help the needy? Likely all of these factors and more.

~

John Davison Rockefeller, the guiding force behind the Standard Oil Company, was a man in a hurry. From modest beginnings, he made his first million dollars at age 33. Those who knew him best claim he had an absolute magnet-affinity for making money ... and for giving it away.

In his lifetime, he contributed more money than any other individual. It is hard to determine precisely the exact amount, but likely it's in excess of $600 million.

Where was the seed planted? What was the motivating force?

Rockefeller was a tither. Even as a teenager with meager earnings – and at times he was virtually penniless – he gave away one-tenth of his income. So the pattern was established early.

But some of his closest associates say it was a health scare, about the time Rockefeller made his first million, that drove him to philanthropy.

Informing the young millionaire he was desperately ill, Rockefeller's doctor recommended acidulated milk and crackers, a diet Rockefeller adhered to for the next seven decades of his life (perhaps explaining his typically unhappy and unpleasant countenance).

It was at this point that John D. Rockefeller became a committed giver. An unrelenting giver.

He even had his servant fill his pockets each morning with fifty dimes, to be presented to strangers as he walked to work. On special occasions, the dimes were changed to silver dollars.

His giving was ceaseless, for a variety of causes and to countless institutions and organizations. Was this simply a continuation of a life-long habit? Was there perhaps a secret covenant made with his God, a pact made after hearing his doctor's report?

~

What motivates large gifts? What are the psychological factors, the pressures, the social imperatives that drive men and women to make gifts of consequential size? Gifts of a million dollars or more. The answer is complex, a puzzle. The plain fact is that probably no single factor is the overriding determinant in making the decision. More than likely it's a combination of feelings, timing, past giving experience, and the motivation and exigency of the moment. Perhaps sheer serendipity.

Why does Alex Spanos, a brilliant West Coast apartment builder, give away millions to a variety of institutions, but refuse to give to a certain local group?

Why did he recently give $250,000 to a museum he had never visited and in response to a telephone call from someone he didn't know?

Why did Marianne McDonald give over $1 million to the esoteric and little known *Thesaurus Linguae Graecae* program at the University of California?

What prompted Arthur Rubloff to give $5 million to a university he never attended?

And Dmitri George, why did he give $1 million to a Chicago hospital?

It can't be simply that these people have the ability to give. Many have the means, but still don't give.

How do you find the "right button?" And when you do, how do you most effectively push it? Solving this riddle has led me on an incredible odyssey.

Join me now on this journey. But I implore you to keep an open mind – much of what you're about to read will shatter some "proven" principles. You may well have to let go of practices you hold dear to your heart.

Like Alice's White Rabbit, putting on his spectacles: "'Where shall I begin please, Your Majesty?' The King looked at him very gravely and replied. 'Begin at the beginning ... and go on 'til you come to the end ... then stop.'"

Let us begin the journey.

2

WHY PEOPLE GIVE

"We would often be ashamed of our finest actions if the world understood all the motives which produce them. There are countless actions and decisions which appear ridiculous, whose hidden motives are wise and weighty. What thoughts and drives, what influences, what past experiences, what inner-most feelings motivate the action?"

– Francis De La Rochefoucauld
Maxims

It's quite clear there isn't any single reason why people give. My interviewing shows that in most cases, donors themselves can't pinpoint their prime motivation. It is puzzling, complex, and often confluent.

But one thing is certain. People do not give because organizations have needs, whether for renovation, equipment, or to overcome a deficit.

In fact, donors run away from "needs." They hide from the institution that isn't financially stable, opting instead for heroic, exciting programs.

Alex Spanos, a man of strong feelings with an opinion on just about everything, is one of the largest apartment builders in the world. He's considered to be one of the wealthiest Greeks in the U.S. And there are countless wealthy Greeks in this country!

Spanos tells me how a hospital approached him to give $1 million for an alcoholic treatment center. If he gave, the center would bear his name. All well and good, except for one thing. The project had no appeal to Spanos – none at all.

"I know there's a need, especially in that area," he tells me. "But for one thing, I don't drink. That kind of a center has no meaning for me. But I do respect the hospital, so I gave them $250,000 and suggested they name it for Betty Ford, the former President's wife. That's what they did, and they raised a lot of money."

Spanos goes on to say: "I never give because I think there's a need. There are lots of needs. I give because it's a program I'm interested in and I think

I can make a real difference."

If organizational needs fail to move donors, then what are some key motivations?

I found that among large givers, there is the strong sense of duty. Often, these individuals feel they have been blessed with money – not always of their making. They believe they have a responsibility to use it and to give it away wisely.

Cyril Magnin, who single-handedly built the 32-store chain, J. Magnin, put it this way: "Great wealth carries great responsibility – a duty. I don't have as much money as others, but what I do have I give away. I've received so much, so very much, and this is a way of helping pay it back."

Magnin then stopped. There was a long pause that seemed like minutes. At last he looked at me, eyes moist. "I have been very fortunate in my life. Ultra-lucky. I feel everyone should give back a good portion of what they receive."

Virginia Piper was given the responsibility for continuing her husband's philanthropy. He was Paul Galvin, the founder of Motorola. Virginia was determined to continue his good work but to do it in her own way and for the organizations she was most interested in.

"I learned a lot from my husband's giving,"

she said. "He felt that what he had on earth had been entrusted to him by God. He felt the responsibility. He was committed to repaying God's gift. I feel the same way – that I've been put here to use the money I have available to do the best work I can."

Louise M. Davies, the wife of oil magnate, Ralph Davies, gave generously to a range of institutions in San Francisco. The symphony hall in that city bears her name.

Davies clearly felt that giving was an obligation. She believed everyone should give. "I remember when I was a Girl Scout," Davies said. "We had to make a fire by rubbing two sticks together – and then we blew and blew, coaxing the spark to a flame. We're all born with a spark, it just takes a little coaxing to get the flame."

Other million dollar donors seem to have been born with the *need* to give. Leo Roon, founder of the Nuodex Products Company, was a preeminent figure in the field of chemical engineering.

There was money in the family, but not very much. When he graduated from high school, Leo won a small cash prize for excellence. He kept none of it for himself, choosing to give it to the uncle who raised him and a few friends.

"Even when I just started in business and things weren't going that well, my company donated more than was deductible by law. It was just something I wanted to do and expected that any good citizen would wish to do." In his lifetime, Leo Roon gave away over $100 million.

Still other million dollar donors are convinced their "good works" will earn them God's special blessing.

When W. Clement Stone made a gift, he felt he was doing the Lord's work in sharing his time, expertise, and wealth. "A spiritual influence is always present in my giving," he said. "When I give, I am directed."

Likewise, there was a spiritual motivation to most of Foster McGaw's giving. He was the founder of the American Hospital Supply Company.

When Foster and his wife gave $1 million each to 32 small colleges, one of the criteria was that the school represent the best in Christian ethics – a code the McGaws believed in. The seed was planted firmly by McGaw's father, a Presbyterian missionary.

Then there are other million dollar donors whose motivation comes from a very specific experience in their life.

Amon Carter, Jr., whose father was publisher of the influential *Star-Telegram* newspaper in Fort Worth, Texas, never forgot the concerned – almost tender – treatment he received in his youth from a YMCA director.

He gave generously to countless organizations and projects, but nothing was closer to his heart than the Y.

James N. Gamble, the grandson of the founder of Proctor & Gamble, and a man who brings total dedication and commitment to any cause he represents, expresses yet another reason why people give. He contends there's a great deal of giving by association.

"People enjoy being a part of 'the club,' being associated with prominent men and women who are giving to the same cause," he says.

And my interviewing bears this out. Very few donors enjoy the independent route – giving to an unpopular cause or a highly experimental project. They much prefer the more accepted organization.

Other donors are lured by the possibility of having a lasting impact. They see great visions and have bold dreams.

Stanley Marcus, scion of a huge retail chain,

Neiman Marcus, and a frequent contributor of $1 million gifts, told me: "I want my gift to count for something. I want to know that what I do can possibly change the lives of thousands. I want to know that I have made a difference. I have done something no one else could have done."

Even though it's hard to identify the precise motivation of a million dollar donor, a few insights about the process of giving do emerge:

• For most people, giving is not rational. Some I interviewed characterized it as being close to a love affair. It is emotional. "I love this place and I love what they are trying to do. It's exciting, and it appeals to me."

• Passion, rather than reason, rules. Not many people compile a list of the institutions seeking their help and then logically weigh the pros and cons of each.

• I'm also convinced that people do not give for tax reasons (more about that later). Although obviously, if there is a tax advantage, that is an added bonus.

• Million dollar givers have a history with the organizations they support. There is virtually no evidence they make a gift in the range of $1 million without any prior experience with the institution itself.

• From my interviews, it's also quite clear that giving is a habit. When a large gift is made to an institution, it will likely not be the last. It will usually be followed by many others – often of increased size.

• And, lastly, I examined carefully those who gave the $1 million gifts. In virtually all cases, the gift was made only after being directly *asked* to do so.

This may be thought unduly basic. But the fundamental verity of securing the gift, upon which all else is predicated, is that you must ask.

Always remember this glaring truth: a cause will be hurt more by those who would have said *yes* but weren't asked, than by those who say *no*.

3

WHEN THEY DON'T BELIEVE, THEY WON'T GIVE

"We make a living by what we get, but we make life of what we give."

– Winston Churchill

Arthur Rubloff amassed a fortune with Chicago real estate. He may have had a heart of gold, but when you sat across the desk from him, he could be plenty tough.

"This fundraiser comes in and is doing a real thing on me," he said in his inimitably gruff way. "But I'm just not interested in what his organization is trying to accomplish. Nothing he can say or do will motivate me to give, not even a small gift. Finally I get tired of listening and ask him to take a walk."

To those who make the really large gift, there has to be an unswerving belief in the objectives and the mission of the institution. No single factor rated higher, or was considered of greater consequence. This takes precedence over everything.

No matter how tantalizing the project, no matter how persuasive the caller, no matter how distinguished the organization, an indefatigable belief in the work and role of the organization is absolutely essential.

"The mission is crucial as far as I am concerned," said Edwin Whitehead, who with his father started Technicon Corporation and later founded the Whitehead Institute at MIT. "I don't care who calls on me, the mission is first."

Whitehead expected uncompromising quality and the highest of standards in the institutions he supported. He looked for long term goals. But first and foremost, he had to identify with the mission.

Roberta Deree thinks about the many projects she and her husband could have supported over the years. William Deree was born in Greece and there was no lack of programs there or in this country which needed help.

An astute businessman with the magic touch for real estate, Deree was wealthy, generous, and accessible. He served on many boards and made a number of gifts, but nothing as substantial as his philanthropy to the American College of Greece.

Mrs. Deree is certain that what attracted her husband to the College was its vital mission. It was something he understood and believed in.

W. Clement Stone put it this way: "All I want to do is to change the world for now and for all generations. In my giving, I'm eager to support organizations that have the same kind of mission I do. I wouldn't consider giving to something I didn't believe in. Not even a small gift."

To Leo Roon, making a gift was inconceivable if he didn't believe strongly in the institution and its mission. "I might make a small donation if a friend or a member of my family was involved. But I have to find something compelling in the program and its objectives before I make a significant gift."

Significant gifts are not made to insignificant projects. Nor to institutions whose mission and objectives aren't in harmony with that of the donor.

And note this well. Big and bold programs sell. Major donors want to soar to heights others have not reached, or cannot reach. They give to dreams and visions that glow.

Marianne McDonald's father founded Zenith Radio Corporation. She feels she is a generous giver, but there must be a sympathetic congruence before she makes a gift.

"There is nothing that could move me to making a large gift if I don't believe in the mission of the organization and its significance," says Marianne, whose sizable gift built the McDonald Center for Substance Abuse on the campus of Scripps Memorial Hospital.

For those organizations with compelling missions, someone is out there ready to give. He or she is in fact waiting to be asked and has the resources to make a gift of consequence.

Sell your mission with the greatest ardor possible. Only when you feel you have accomplished this are you ready to talk about the campaign program or the specific project.

4

STAFF GIVES INSPIRATION AND LIGHTS THE WAY

"A leader has the power to persuade and motivate others to heights believed to be unreachable."

– James Lewis Russell

Not of equal importance with the mission of the organization, but ranking quite high among the factors considered important to large donors, is the management of the institution.

Strong staff attracts strong boards. One begets the other. One challenges and stimulates the other. It's synergy.

The weak and financially unstable institution is most often led by weak and ineffective staff, who in turn attract members cut from the same cloth.

High-powered, decisive men and women aren't inspired by weak staff.

Before making a gift, W. Clement Stone looked first to see that the institution was properly staffed and managed. Stone, the guru of the Positive Mental Attitude – the person who invented it – gave away $200 million in his lifetime.

"I think the management is the most important thing," he said. "That's what gets my greatest attention. I won't give to a program unless I feel it can be properly managed."

Clement Stone was a fascinating giver. There appeared to be no reason or rhythm to the pattern of his philanthropy.

But look closer and you'll see he consistently bet on people. If he didn't have full confidence and trust in the chief staff person, he wasn't likely to give. On the other hand, if he found the staff vital and effective, there was a burst of electricity — and the organization was likely to receive a large gift. A very large gift!

Interlochen is now considered one of the important summer music camps in the nation. It would be fair to say that before Stone got involved, it didn't really amount to much. He breathed life into the program, and gave millions of dollars.

What sparked his commitment and dedication? What inspired that whirlwind of activity and money. Music wasn't even a great interest.

Here's what Clement Stone told me: "It was the dynamic leadership and vision of the staff – that's what got me going and kept me interested."

Dr. Kenneth Chorley is considered to be the genius behind Colonial Williamsburg. He was the CEO hired by David Rockefeller to head the planning and implement the program for Colonial Williamsburg.

It was the Rockefeller millions that made it possible, but it was Chorley's inspiration and encouragement which made it happen.

I spoke to David Rockefeller about this partnership. "Dad had the dream, but Ken Chorley gave him the inspiration," he said. "The money itself would have meant nothing without the leadership Chorley provided."

Virginia Piper gave away millions. She's now in heaven helping the angels direct their good deeds. At her death, she created the largest foundation in Arizona.

Virginia's philanthropy was almost always emotional and spontaneous. But she felt strongly about the role of the staff. "When I evaluate a gift to an organization," she said, "I feel the management has to be outstanding. I have to believe in them. And one follows the other – if there's a good manager, there's always a good and strong board. Always."

"It's not hard to explain," says Mrs. William Deree. Her husband gave $1.5 million to the American College of Greece. William Deree had the financial resources. His wife, Roberta, provided the inspiration and encouragement which made the gift possible.

William Deree was passionately Greek. That helps explain his gift to an institution with a Greek heritage. But why to the American College of Greece? Why not to the Greek Orthodox Church? Or the Greek Welfare Foundation? Or St. Basil's Academy? Or Hellenic College?

He was on the board or a leader in each one of these organizations. The key for unlocking the gift was the staff leadership, the president of the American College.

"Bill had this tremendous regard for the president – his integrity and the feeling that he's a strong captain of the ship," says Roberta. "I know the gift finally went to the College for that reason."

When staff leadership is right, key volunteers can always be counted on to follow. The president of the college, the administrator of the hospital, the executive director of the organization – their roles are critical.

For the mega donor, it's an emphatic case of: The effectiveness of your management speaks so loudly, I can't hear what you say about your fundraising program.

This helps explain why staff can be so effective in securing the large gift. Major donors respond to staff. They give to vital, strong, dynamic staffs. And they make gifts far beyond what they might have initially considered.

In fact, of the donors I interviewed, their million dollar gifts were made to institutions where there was an unbreakable bond of regard and respect between them and the chief staff person.

There wasn't one exception.

5

TAX IS LITTLE INCENTIVE

"Gain all you can, save all you can, give all you can."

– John Wesley

Pick up any organizational brochure or piece of campaign literature. The chances are almost certain there will be a major reference to the tax deductibility of a gift. And there's often a prominent reference to it in written and verbal presentations to potential major donors.

But how significant is the matter of tax deductibility? Not very, according to my interviews.

"I don't give much thought to the tax consideration," Cyril Magnin told me. "I get paid off in the satisfaction of knowing I'm doing something that is good."

When Dmitri George, a Chicago developer who transforms apartment buildings to condominiums, made his million-dollar gift to a hospital, the tax implication wasn't a factor at all.

His father had received excellent care following a difficult heart operation. Mr. George made the gift to show his appreciation.

By his own estimates, Leo Roon gave away $100 million in his lifetime. And that didn't even count gifts that weren't tax-deductible.

"I think a person who really enjoys giving doesn't worry much about the taxes," said Roon. "There was a young boy, a cerebral palsy victim, who was a great friend of my grandson's.

"I knew he was going to have a terrible time in life and so I decided to establish a trust for him. It amounts to about $100,000. I'll tell you, that gives me just about as much satisfaction as any gift I've ever made."

Roon went on to say: "I declare everything I can. But tax isn't a major factor, ever. When Ann and I see a need that's important, we give."

Like Roon, every major donor takes full advantage of the tax laws. Of course! But it's doubtful tax appreciably affects the philanthropic pattern of major donors. Donors give – tax advantage or not. The fact that the government participates in the giving encourages the donor to do even more.

George Pardee, who along with his father and brothers were pioneers in turning Las Vegas' dirt roads into communities, fit this category.

Here's what he told me: "There are several things that affect my giving in a major way. The tax consideration is always a factor, but it's not the first thing I think about."

Louise M. Davies had a banker and an attorney who worked with her in her tax planning. She listened to them. But she still did as she pleased. "Tax is certainly not a factor for me," she said. "It really isn't. I always make the gift first, and then worry about the tax."

Consider this, too. Most of the major donors give beyond the maximum limit. Dorothy Simmerly considers taxes when giving, but points out that generally it doesn't do any good. She gives far beyond the deductibility limit.

Arthur Rubloff was another who exceeded the deductible amount allowed by law. "I disregard the tax question completely," he said. "It has no relevancy in determining whether I would make a gift or not."

In interview after interview, tax was played down, if not dismissed, by the mega givers. Do I take that at face value? I do!

By training, I am a listener. In a major way, that's how I make my living. Listening.

With each million-dollar donor, I explored the matter of taxes. Scrutinized. Poked and probed. Inquired in a variety of ways. I am convinced the responses were open, direct, and candid. And from the heart.

On top of all of that, most of the people I interviewed were friends, and if not friends at least men or women I felt I knew well. They had nothing to prove – not to me, not to anyone.

In my mind, the evidence is clear and incontestable. You don't sell a major donor by talking about the tax advantages.

6

ARE YOU DOZING THROUGH A CHANGING MARKET?

"Every donor should look to his own purpose and problems, which are not necessarily those of the institution. Even in philanthropy, the customer is usually right, and his judgment can be just as thoughtful, long range, and in the public interest as those of the recipient. Often more so."

– Kenneth Patrick

Lorillard, the tobacco company, was having a disastrous time promoting its full-flavored cigarettes.

Consumer attitudes about smoking were changing. People were kicking the habit. Even those who continued to smoke began looking at the tar numbers.

But Lorillard continued its heavy promotion of macho men, tattoos, western scenes – the whole works. Their sales plummeted. Finally, they conducted a market study.

"Those tests opened our eyes," recounts Curt Judge, head of Lorillard. "We got wise enough to say, Hell, let's give them what they want."

What consumers wanted were lower tar cigarettes. Lorillard introduced Newport, True, and Satin and soon after turned its losses into profits.

Two hundred years earlier, Benjamin Franklin had a similar problem selling his product. To induce France to join the young colony in its fight against England, a stream of official representatives called on the French.

They tried to convince the French that their participation in the war would be to their commercial advantage and enhance their trade and business. The new country would import only from France.

It was to no avail. The French were unmoved.

Franklin knew better. He understood the French were a passionate people, moved more by their heart than their pocket.

"France is truly a generous nation and

gracious people, fond of glory, and particularly interested in protecting the oppressed," he said.

Among his many other talents, Franklin was a master marketer. He sold the French on helping the underdog, the oppressed. He sold liberty and honor. And France joined the Revolution.

Securing a large gift is often a case of good marketing. It's the gracious art of helping men and women realize their noblest aspirations.

But to win them to your cause you must follow the time-tested marketing adage – give them more and more of what they want and less and less of what they don't want.

That doesn't mean you settle for a designated gift that isn't relevant to your organization's mission or one not in keeping with the program or the campaign.

Good marketing means melding your passion and dream to the donor's inner-most desire. And that's something requiring proper interpretation and effective persuasion.

And you listen. You hear what the donor's hopes and aspirations are for the organization.

Homer Watkins, a Los Angeles developer of shopping centers, says he is tired of organizations trying to sell him their bill of goods. "They come marching in here with their ideas and their fancy proposals," he says.

"They don't ask what I'm interested in. They're only concerned with telling me what they want me to buy. It is impossible for me to get involved in that kind of a situation."

As Watkins makes clear, too often in fundraising the programs that might be the most important to your organization are irrelevant to the major donor.

A favorite story of Dale Carnegie's was recounting how he went fishing in Maine every summer. "I'm very fond of strawberries and cream," he said.

"But I find for some strange reason, fish prefer worms. I don't bait the hook with strawberries and cream. Rather, I dangle a worm or a grasshopper in front of the fish and I say – wouldn't you like to have that?"

Why not use the same common sense as Dale Carnegie when you are fishing for a gift.

7

THE BUCK STARTS WITH THE BOARD

"Every profession is a conspiracy against
the laity."
                              – George Bernard Shaw

For years, Walter A. Haas, Jr. headed what
was considered the world's most successful gar-
ment manufacturer, Levi Strauss & Co. The company was founded by his great grand uncle.

Haas was a recognized leader in the business
community, locally and internationally. He was a
strong advocate of volunteerism and played a
vital volunteer role his entire adult life.

An active giver in the Jewish community, Haas

was equally generous to a wide range of organizations and institutions. His greatest enthusiasm and support, however, was reserved for the University of California, Berkeley.

About one thing, Haas was unforgiving. He said serving on an organization's board of directors carries with it a financial responsibility.

"Someone like me shouldn't serve on a board without supporting it financially," he told me. "Every board member should give. It's just like being on the board of a corporation, you should own a few shares of stock."

Serving on the board of an organization is a high calling and implies a major responsibility and commitment. Brown University's former president, Henry Wriston, originated the three venerable "Ws" years ago. They are just as relevant today. Perhaps more so.

Dr. Wriston established for his trustees three criteria – work, wealth, and wisdom. Every institutional administrator fervently longs for trustees who can bring a matched set of all three "Ws."

Two of the three should be mandatory. And if a trustee brings only one "W," the chances are fairly certain his or her effectiveness will be severely limited.

I have added a fourth W – Wallop. You want

board members of great influence – within the community and with the organization's constituency.

Louise Davies, whose generosity provided the great thrust in constructing the magnificent performing arts center in San Francisco, made no bones about the role of board members.

"If you serve on the board, you're expected to give," she said. "You shouldn't be a director unless you are prepared to give. Otherwise, get out of the way so somebody else can serve. "

Investment banker Joe Riggs (not his real name) tells me about his $5 million gift to the Smithsonian Institute. It is the largest gift he has ever made.

"What prompted you to make such a gift?" I ask.

"If you're on the Smithsonian Board as I am, you're simply expected to give. No one questions it. And, by the way, mine wasn't the largest gift."

I probe further. "What about other institutions, perhaps less prestigious than the Smithsonian? "Should board members there be expected to give too?"

"It's all the same," Riggs replies. "If you're a trustee, you should be expected to give as much as you can – both annually and for special campaigns. Some may not be able to do as much as others. But if you're a board member, you give. Period."

Leo Beranek, co-founder of one of the world's largest acoustical consulting firms, tells how he's been interested in music since he was 10 or 11. His gift to the Boston Symphony – the largest it had received up to that time – was an easy decision.

"It was very natural for me to be interested in our symphony. I was on the board for almost 15 years and as a director, I felt encouraged to give a little bit more money," he said.

"When I was asked to chair the resources committee, I felt I had to set a good example. If I hadn't been as heavily involved, I wouldn't have done as much."

~

Direct involvement in a program isn't a prerequisite for major giving. Nor is it a guarantee. On the other hand, involvement is unquestionably an important motivating factor.

Familiarity breeds favorability is a truism you can count on "with the calm confidence of a Christian with four aces," to use Mark Twain's words.

And if you need one last piece of evidence that commitment follows involvement, here it is. Last year, two out of every three persons who gave $1 million gifts (or more) were on the board of directors of the recipient institution.

Case closed.

8

GO FOR
THE CHALLENGE

"Here's the challenge. Give an ear. Heed the
message. I warrant there's vinegar and pepper in it.
Aye, the challenge ignites the heart."

– Shakespeare

I learned my early lessons in fundraising from
some wonderful volunteers and a number of major donors. They were all great teachers.

Clement Stone was one of them. Much of his
philanthropy was in the form of challenge gifts,
motivating others to do more and reach higher.

"I most often make challenge gifts," Stone
told me. "I really believe this encourages others."
He cited this instance.

"On one of my projects, we were coming near the end of the program," he said, "and the organization hadn't raised the money to meet my challenge. 'Look, a deal's a deal,' I told them. 'If you don't raise it, you don't get my gift.' In a week they went out and raised the whole amount, and then some. I've been an exponent of the challenge gift for years."

But surprisingly, challenge gifts, at least on the surface, aren't as important to mega givers as I had thought.

"I don't worry much about what others give," said Cyril Magnin. "If I'm interested in the program, I'm interested. If not, the challenge doesn't motivate me. I think that what others do is up to them."

Homer Watkins is even more direct. "I don't care what others do," he says. "I wouldn't change my thinking about a gift because of a challenge. And I don't think it motivates others either."

San Diego Chargers owner Alex Spanos agrees. He says a challenge gift has never spurred him to make a sizable gift. "Matching someone's gift means nothing to me," he says. "I like being the one who makes the large gift and does the challenging."

Spanos admits, however, that he's likelier to

participate if he knows others are supporting the program heavily.

Still, in my experience, I find the challenge gift to be a valuable concept. Let me give you an example. One of many.

In a college campaign I was involved with, we visited the largest potential donor first. We had prepared well. It was an excellent presentation. The only problem was that the donor had pretty much made up his mind what to give.

It was a good gift, but only about half of what we hoped for. Before leaving the donor, we suggested he give what he had planned, but consider doubling the gift if the campaign was successful. He agreed.

We announced this "added" gift that would be forthcoming if everyone did their share. The campaign exceeded its goal and we received the bonus.

DeWitt Wallace and his wife Lila Acheson were the founders of *Reader's Digest*. Some years ago, they agreed to give the Girls Clubs of America (now Girls, Inc.) $1 million if they raised an equal amount.

The organization had just completed a successful campaign several years earlier, but Wallace's challenge gift encouraged them to start again. They did, and were successful. I doubt it would have happened without the challenge.

Despite what mega givers say, it is indisputable that in countless campaigns, a challenge has helped put the program over.

9

NAMING OPPORTUNITIES ARE GOLDEN OPPORTUNIES

" Living is the act of loving.
Loving is the act of caring.
Caring is the act of sharing.
Sharing is the act of living."

– Author Unknown

When asked whether memorial giving is an incentive for them, many of the million dollar donors I interviewed said it was not.

Still, as the following examples make clear, memorial giving can be a strong motivating force.

In some families, there is a heritage of giving. From one generation to another, the tradition is handed down. In these instances the children will often memorialize their parents.

I think of DeWitt Wallace and his wife who were generous in extraordinary proportions. There were many gifts of a million dollars or more, and often they allowed their names to memorialize the gift. In their early philanthropy, however, they especially honored Mr. Wallace's father, a missionary.

Another example that comes to mind is John Detwiler, a man who had a great love for the sea.

Detwiler had long planned a spectacular two weeks of scuba diving on the remote island of Palowan.

Three weeks after graduating from medical school, his dream became a reality. But on the first day of that fateful adventure, while exploring a sunken freighter, Detwiler disappeared.

Crews searched for him for two days before finally giving up. Five days later his body washed ashore. He had drifted fifteen miles.

It had been Detwiler's dream to one day build and equip a Chinese junk to do medical missionary work in the needy areas of the Southern Philippines.

To honor the memory of this young doctor,

and to fulfill the lost promise of medical help, his parents gave $1 million to establish a medical school at the Philippine Union College.

Detwiler's father, Howard, also a physician, has a great love for the Filipino people. His thought in making the gift was to continue the unfulfilled work of his son. It was a memorial gift, no doubt about it. And one with a deeply moving and spiritual basis.

Institutions have become tastefully ingenious about memorializing gifts. Buildings are an obvious possibility. Endowing chairs at a university. Hospital rooms or entire wings. YMCA swimming pools. Individual chairs in an auditorium.

The Phoenix Symphony endowed each of the 88 keys of the new Steinway piano. The piano honored Dayton Fowler Grafman, chairman of the board – at $5,000 a key.

At Penn State University, all the positions on the football team are endowed (sorry, every position – even nose tackle – is taken).

In the case of the National College of Education in Evanston, Illinois, all of the buildings were already named. During a campaign for endowment, Foster McGaw, founder and guiding force behind the American Hospital Supply Company, was approached for a major gift. He gave over $4 million to the endowment program.

However, there was nothing left to name. To honor the contribution, the College built a small gatepost at its main entrance to the campus and named it in honor of Mr. McGaw. Not a wall, just a gate and post. But it was indeed a memorable way to honor a special benefactor.

There are times, though, when an institution draws the line. Samuel Gomberg offered to give $10,000 for every urinal New York University would name in his honor. The University respectfully declined the invitation!

The Right Person Should Ask

10

THE RIGHT PERSON SHOULD ASK

"Success is achieved by those who try and those who ask."

– W. Clement Stone

There can be no mistake, the quintessence of successful fundraising is the careful and sometimes imaginative matching of askers to givers.

But who precisely is the right person to do the asking? From my observation, the old adage of peer-on-peer may not necessarily be the only answer. Indeed it may not be an answer at all.

This represents a great departure from what has been a sound and long-cherished concept. Namely that volunteers, particularly peers of the prospect, are the most effective solicitors.

But according to my research, that's not always the case. Every situation is an opportunity for a highly thought-out and considered plan.

Dorothy Simmerly gave the largest gift to a national campaign for the Episcopal church. The person who made the call, who asked for the gift, was the national head of the church, the Archbishop.

"It was the first time I'd met him," she said. "I was greatly impressed with his tremendous energy and vision. I was sold from the beginning and I must say, it felt good being called on by the highest man in the Church."

Dortch Oldham is one of Nashville's most respected citizens. A leader, a doer, a giver. Before selling it to the Times Mirror company, Oldham owned the Southwestern Corp., a company that employs college students each summer to sell a variety of books door to door.

Oldham has great regard for the president of his alma mater. That was an important element in his making several million-dollar gifts to Richmond University.

He says there isn't anyone who can raise money like the chief staff person. It's a key factor, according to Oldham.

Arthur Rubloff was a rags-to-riches story and a chronic giver. Some say he owned most of downtown Chicago, and a suburb or two. That's an overstatement, of course. But not by much.

Rubloff gave $5 million to both the University of Chicago and Northwestern University. Here's what he told me about those gifts. "It wasn't a case of special loyalty to either institution – they're both distinguished universities. I didn't attend either.

"The president of each called on me and, for these two projects, I think the president was the right person. Maybe I wouldn't have reacted as well to a volunteer."

But other million dollar donors don't seem to care who calls on them, so long as it's someone they respect.

"It's important who asks for the gift," says venture capitalist, Robert Saligman. "But to me it doesn't matter if it's a staff person, a volunteer, or a friend. It just needs to be someone I respect."

Using practically the same words, here's what Leo Roon had to say on the subject. "It can be a staff person or a board member – that doesn't really matter, just so I have a high regard for them.

It doesn't have to be a peer, either, or someone who will give as much as I will."

It was the same for W. Clement Stone. "When [naming one of Chicago's leading industrialists] walks in the door and says 'Clem, I really need your help,' you can bet I always make a gift. But the right staff member can do a good job, too."

One thing that may surprise you is that friendship with the solicitor doesn't necessarily play a pivotal role.

"Once in a while a close friend will call on me and because of our relationship," says Leo Beranek. "I feel compelled to do something. But if it's an organization I'm not particularly interested in, it will be a very small gift, a token, a couple thousand dollars."

Leo Roon concurred: "If a friend asks me for a gift and I'm not especially interested in the organization, chances are I'll do something. But I certainly won't make a large gift to the organization."

And Cyril Magnin agreed: "It is the project that attracts me, that compels me. Not the person. Even if a friend, a dear friend, called on me, it wouldn't make any difference. I've learned to give only to programs where I feel my help can make a difference."

What my interviews show is this. The solicitor can be a staff person, a volunteer, or a peer. Any of them, as long as they command respect. But you must know your prospect well enough to identify just who the right person is.

Where a personal friend or peer can make a difference is in securing the appointment with the prospect. It is a plain fact of fundraising that it's often far more difficult to get an appointment than the gift.

The known philanthropist has been called on before. Many times. And faced with the never-ending pleading for gifts, he has developed a hide the thickness of a rhinoceros. Getting the interview can be the most important strategy of all.

Whenever possible, have a peer or a friend call for the visit. Have them accompany you on the call, along with a staff person. That can be a formidable combination. I call it the *Magic Partnership*. The peer needn't say much. Have the staff person do the talking, even ask for the gift.

Running through most of my interviews is another thread that refutes what has been said so often it has become gospel – that two people can make an effective call, but more than two can overwhelm.

Not true!

I find it can be very persuasive and impressive to have three or four attend one of the early sessions with a donor. Try it. A friend, the chief executive officer, the chairman of the campaign, and a person who has made a gift at the level you seek. (I say take the Marching Band if you think it will help!)

The prospective donor knows he's in for a formidable time, but somehow seems to enjoy the fuss.

He is impressed that so many important people are taking time to make the call. It must be important to them. It must be an important program. It must be a gift at an important level they are seeking.

Just make sure you carefully orchestrate the discussion so there's a role for everyone. That's important.

There's one last hoary tale I'd like to lay permanently to rest. It holds that the person who solicits should have already made a gift equal to the one he or she will be asking for.

Over the years, this axiom has been repeated so often it's now considered Holy Grail. But it's rubbish!

Here's the rule you must follow. It is irrefutable.

The person asking for the gift must have made his own gift, and it must be at a tiptoe level. If it is a sacrificial gift, or the largest he has ever made to anything, all the better. But it doesn't have to be equal to the prospect's anticipated gift.

One closing note. It is interesting that of all the million dollar gifts I reviewed, only one presentation was made at lunch. There is no scientific data to substantiate this, but a meal – with all of the clang and clatter, table-hopping, and irrelevant chatter – takes away measurably from the focus of the meeting

A waiter asking for the dessert order at precisely the wrong time can cause an unnerving interruption. While you may savor a fine raspberry torte, the magic moment can be lost forever.

11

THE SPOUSE COUNTS

> "When I talk with mothers and fathers, I tell them to give their time to great causes. Let their candle burn at both ends if necessary. Teach your children that it will provide a dazzling light for others to follow. And remember, God divided the hand into fingers so that the money can slip through to the church and the needy."
>
> – Martin Luther

It's a statistical fact that women live longer than men (it's said that no one lives longer than a widow who has named your organization in her will).

Don't miss an opportunity. During the life of the wealthy man who serves on your board, be certain his wife is invited, whenever possible, to participate in programs and activities. Be sure she receives information, and is called on.

Create opportunities for the two of them to join in organizational events, annual meetings, retreats. When the man sits on the dais or is recognized for his leadership or a gift, give his wife equal attention. It is the right thing to do. And it will pay.

And if the man precedes his wife, consider adding her to the board. His dedication to the organization will continue through her. And his benevolences.

You don't even have to wait long before making the widow a part of your organization or asking for a gift (see Chapter 13, *Seize the Magic Moment*). It may be too late if you do.

Involve her in the program as soon as possible. It will pay remarkable results to your organization and, at the same time, help the widow through her bereavement.

Herbert Cummings was one of the great philanthropists and volunteers of Phoenix. There was no one more highly respected. Of all the organizations he supported, his most abiding love, by far, was for Scottsdale Memorial Hospital.

When he died, hospital officials felt they should wait "a respectful" amount of time before asking Deanna, his wife, for a memorial gift to honor Herb. An appropriate waiting period is of course a matter of subjective judgment and discretion. Some would say, civility.

The Museum in Phoenix didn't wait. Soon after Herb's death, they asked for a gift and got it. At the same time, they asked her to become a member of their board. And she did.

Nor did those at Presbyterian-St. Luke's (Chicago) wait to ask Patti Gerber for a gift after her husband's passing. Patti's money came from her family's interest in wholesale plumbing products. She gave $5 million as a memorial to him.

I will admit this gift surprised me. I knew for a fact that Lake Forest Hospital was Patti's regular hospital. That's where the kids were born. That's where the family was always treated. I asked her why she did it.

"A few days after my husband died," Patti tells me, "some friends on the board at Presbyterian St. Luke's came by and asked me to make a gift to the Hospital in honor of my husband.

"I didn't know anything about their hospital and never used it. But I thought it was a good idea. I wanted desperately to do something. No one from Lake Forest Hospital came by to ask for a gift."

Husbands and wives discuss their philanthropy. Major gifts are almost always made in joint agreement. Oh, there may be an exception, but don't count on it.

Dr. Cecil Green, co-founder of Texas Instruments, gave away well over $200 million in his lifetime. In all cases he conferred with his wife Ida before making the final decision. Most of the gifts were designated as coming from both Cecil and Ida Green. A partnership of giving.

Leo Beranek says he always talks to his wife about their gifts. And all of the gifts are given in both names.

Alex Spanos discusses all of his giving with his wife, Faye.

The same dynamic applies when the wife's money is the greater resource (often through inheritance or even a prior divorce), husbands and wives make a joint decision.

But too often, the romancing, the interpretation of the case, the call itself is made on only one – most often the husband. If it truly is a shared decision, and the evidence clearly supports this, then it is imperative you call on the husband and wife together to make the sale.

You'll miss a golden opportunity if you don't.

12

MATERIAL IS IMMATERIAL

"I regard most campaign brochures the same way
I think of the Goodyear Blimp: unmoving, hollow,
and full of hot air."
– Arthur Frantzreb

To give breath and life to the dream, many
organizations start with glorious campaign literature, magnificent brochures, four-color pieces,
catchy and heart-rendering themes. There is blind
embossing and raised relief printing.

But as far as the major donor is concerned, my
interviews and my own experience confirm that
this type of selling is usually ineffective. Often it's
detrimental.

For many major donors, sophisticated or fancy
campaign literature has as much impact as the

sound of one hand clapping.

To a person, the donors I spoke with are unimpressed by handsome brochures, fancy folders, or finely detailed illustrations. A simple presentation is much more respected.

Alex Spanos says that most campaign material is a waste of time. "It really turns me off. The fancier it is, the angrier I get. People tell you that they just throw the stuff in the wastebasket. Well, I do."

Marianne McDonald, who has used her Zenith inheritance for a number of entrepreneurial and philanthropic endeavors, is an attractive, vivacious woman.

She earned a doctorate in Classical Studies and lives on 27 acres in Southern California, along with a horde of children, several peacocks, a number of dogs, and an assortment of other animals and birds of all sizes and varieties.

"Some campaign material really puts me off," says McDonald. "I hate that a lot of money has been spent to convince me of something. All of that fancy stuff is counterproductive."

Arnold Beckman, founder of Beckman Instruments, made a fortune (likely $1 billion) with his innovations. And he gave it all away. He loved to give – but with the sharp eye of an engineer. He carefully analyzed everything – including his philanthropy.

During our visit in his book-lined office, Beckman spotted me eyeing a binder on his desk. It was obviously a proposal. Leather bound, brass corners, and it had Beckman's name in gold leaf on the spine.

"Pretty impressive," I said.

"Trash," he replied. "I wouldn't even look at the pages of something like this. It turns me off. They seem to have enough money if they can put together something like this. Why didn't they just send a trustee or a staff member to tell me the story?"

Well, then, here's the question. How do you get your story across effectively?

For most major donors, you do it as simply as possible. And as personally as possible.

You talk about your institution. Its special mission. How it serves a need unmet by any other organization. How your campaign program can meet both the objectives of the organization and the wishes of the donor.

You talk, but if you are smart, you listen.

After you truly understand the needs and

dreams of the donor, and only after that, are you in a position to present precisely the right campaign material.

Campaign literature is certainly important. It states officially the dimensions of the program. The solicitor should use it to cement in place the oral presentation.

I find the most impressive and effective presentations are typed and placed in a three-ring binder – usually studded with captivating and appropriate photographs. (No one, to my knowledge, has ever thrown away a three-ring binder!)

Among those I interviewed, many made their gift without any campaign material at all. The balance had tailor-made presentations.

"I need to know why they want me to give to their program," said Amon Carter, Jr. "Me, particularly."

And you do that most persuasively with the spoken word.

13

SEIZE THE MAGIC MOMENT

"It is the magic of the program, soaring aspirations and bold challenges, that capture the heart and soul."

– Dr. Robert Schuller

It is best he remain nameless. I think he'd prefer it that way. He's the popular minister of one of our nation's largest Methodist churches.

And just the day before he had learned one of the great lessons of fundraising. The memory was still vivid.

Recently, at a small gathering of ministers he recounted the story. I was there.

The wealthiest member of his congregation, a

widow, was in the hospital – a long-term illness closing in on her. Over a period of three months, the minister made regular calls, at least twice weekly and often more than that.

"Let's be honest, gentlemen," the minister said to the group. "I considered it my pastoral duty to visit with this faithful servant. But I was mindful, too, of her immense wealth and that we were certain to be the beneficiary of her large estate.

"There were no children, no relatives, only her great, abiding love for the church. She often spoke to me, even before her illness, of all she hoped to do for us."

Those around the table clung to the minister's every word.

"I visited her faithfully, week in and week out," he continued. "I brought her spiritual encouragement, often small gifts like stationery, and held her hand while we prayed. It was a ministry of love. She was one of my longtime favorites.

"Finally, after all of that suffering, the end came. She slipped quietly into the night. There would be no more pain."

That was a month before.

"Yesterday," the minister continued, "I found

out from her attorney – also a member of the congregation – about the disposition of her estate. While in the hospital, she had arranged her affairs."

By now, the minister's small audience was riveted

"Well, this gentle soul, one of the most active women in the congregation, left her entire estate to a Midwestern university, her husband's alma mater."

More than a few gasps were heard around the table.

"I was incredulous. And I must admit, I was devastated. What happened? I asked the attorney."

It turns out the priest who was the president of the University came by the hospital one day for a visit.

"He asked her for a gift," the minister said. "That's all he did. He asked. It occurred to me that in all of the time I had known this lady and in all my visits, I never asked for a gift. I took that for granted."

The minister ended his story. It was a teachable moment.

The moral of this story, even to the uninitiated, is clear. But still it remains one of the major stumbling blocks of the fundraiser. You must ask for the order!

It is absolutely amazing what you don't get when you don't ask!

Samuel Skaggs, who helped pioneer the concept of self-service retail stores, gave $1 million to Iliff School of Theology. Earl Wood was the School's director of development, and was responsible for getting the gift.

It was the largest contribution the seminary had ever received. It was also the largest gift Mr. Skaggs had ever given to a United Methodist cause. Later, the inevitable question was asked.

"Mr. Skaggs, you've been a loyal member of the church for years and have been devoted to our work. You've given generously to other organizations. How does it happen that this is the first time you've given this large a gift to a Methodist cause?"

Mr. Skaggs responded without hesitation, "This is the first time anyone ever asked me."

Earl Wood asked for the order.

Sending a letter or telephoning simply won't do. Not for the large gift. That's stating the obvious.

As Harold Seymour put it many years ago,

no one ever got milk from a cow by sending a letter. You put your stool right next to Betsy, stroke her properly, and keep working at it.

And that's how you get a large gift. Lots of stroking, lots of innovative cultivation, and – this is *critical* – the wisdom to seize the magic moment when it presents itself.

14

THE RESPONSE IS SPONTANEOUS

"What great things would you attempt if you knew you could not fail?"

– Robert Fuller

It was a fascinating story.

Alex Spanos lives in Stockton, California – a couple of hours away from San Francisco, if you drive fast.

It's a world away in almost every other respect. Spanos, who parlayed an $800 loan into a mega real estate and development company, tells me about a telephone call he received.

"This lady calls. She says she's on the board of a

museum in San Francisco. Would I be interested in sponsoring their 'Search for Alexander' exhibit."

That's all the caller says. Short and sweet. No mincing of words.

The moment Spanos heard the idea, he was excited. And it will probably surprise you to learn that it took him only a few seconds to decide.

"I thought it was a great idea, and expressed a part of my heritage." On top of that, I was named for Alexander. Everything just fit into place. I don't believe I found out until much later what the cost was – $250,000."

When Spanos told the solicitor he would sponsor the exhibit, there was a l-o-n-g silence. "Am I speaking to Mr. Spanos? Oh, I really am," said the caller.

And then almost in disbelief: "Er, Mr. Spanos, would you be interested in knowing anything more or what the cost would be?"

The gift was made and delivered. On the spot. Spontaneously.

All gifts aren't made that quickly. You can count on that. But it is my experience – confirmed by the million dollar givers – that major philanthropy is spontaneous.

Donors may not make the actual gift or sign

the pledge card for months. But in their minds they have pretty much made their decision to support the program or not.

I'm now convinced that if there's no "immediate click," you probably won't get the gift. There is much truth to the old legal axiom, *to delay is to deny.*

A thoughtful donor will certainly wish to talk to his or her spouse about a gift. If it is in the range of "major proportions," an attorney or accountant will probably be consulted. This takes time. But that's not the kind of delay I refer to.

I have been involved in many campaigns where some of our top prospects have put us off, avoided making a decision, or have indicated we should see them in six months or so.

We hung on to those prospects for dear life. In some cases they were our major hope.

Virtually none of those gifts materialized. Now when I think about it, I realize there wasn't the spark, the excitement. No awe or wonder. No trumpets.

The chances are almost certain you won't receive a meaningful answer or a consequential gift on the first visit. If you do, odds are you could have gotten more!

On the other hand, if you have made several calls, put forth a solid presentation, and still you don't see positive signals, you had better begin formulating a different strategy.

"I'd like to wait until things get better." "Not right now, maybe later." "I'll see what my attorney says and get back to you in a couple of months." These can be sure signs you'd better look for another top prospect. You are most likely to be disappointed.

"I give spontaneously," Marianne McDonald says. "I think most people do.

"I find if I'm spending a great deal of time deciding, I usually end up not giving. When a program is just right for me I feel it immediately."

Louise M. Davies told me about her gift to establish the Center for Performing Arts in San Francisco (now known as the Louise M. Davies Center for the Performing Arts).

"I decided I was going to give as soon as I heard about the project. There was none of that campaign material or a fancy sales call. I pretty much made up my mind on the spot."

Only after she decided did Davies tell her tax advisor and banker what she had done.

Arthur Rubloff was once a pin boy in a bowling alley earning 50 cents a day. That was long before he built one of the largest real estate empires in the country.

"It doesn't really take me much time to decide whether I'm interested in a program," he told me. "As soon as I hear the story, I have a fairly good idea of whether I'm going to give.

"That doesn't mean I'm always right. And certainly I've had some major disappointments with some projects. But I still feel that my initial instincts are right."

Cyril Magnin was first and foremost a tough businessman. He always gave carefully. "I try to make certain the organizations are worthy," he said, "and that my money is being put to the best possible use.

"But there's a definite spontaneity to what I do. It takes me virtually no time to decide whether I'm interested in the program. A bell rings inside. I hear the presentation and almost immediately I decide if I am going to give or not."

Large gifts. Really large gifts. These are given emotionally, not cerebrally. And almost always, the decision is made spontaneously. The final commitment may come later but the spark is ignited early.

15

FIND A WAY TO RECOGNIZE

"You make a decision. You determine what you should do with your life. How much are you willing to sacrifice? How much are you willing to give of yourself, your time, your love, your resources? You give. And you give until the Lord stops giving to you. When you do, you find life has taken on a whole new meaning."

– John Lewis Russell

Cicero wrote two thousand years ago: "In nothing do men more nearly approach the gods than in doing good to their fellow men."

This should be gratification enough, though without question recognition does play an important role for the donor.

History has recorded few truly anonymous gifts. Many benefactors, who pretend anonymity, hide after conferring a gift – much like Virgil's Galatea. She fled ... but only after making certain she had been seen by everyone.

Fred Meier of Grand Rapids, Michigan is a remarkably generous donor to many causes. Recently for the Heart Center at Blodgett Hospital, he made a gift of $10 million. He insisted it be totally anonymous. But he told everyone in town what he had done!

As you would imagine, it's extremely difficult to distinguish between those who want recognition and those who really don't.

On the basis of my interviews, I'm convinced that even though most of the million dollar givers don't expect a cannon-shot display of media and plaques, it does mean a great deal to them to have others know what they've done.

Alex Spanos is clear on the subject of recognition.

"The impact of the gift, the recognition of it, is terribly important to me," he says. "I think if people are honest, I mean really honest, they would admit it's important. There isn't a man alive who doesn't like recognition that comes from giving."

Dmitri George likes attention as well. He told me that after his gift was made, there was no end to the processional from the hospital.

"The architects visited to show me their plans and ask my reaction. The administrator called regularly to keep me informed of the progress of the construction. The director of development wrote me letters and sent clippings. The groundbreaking was a three-ring circus."

And Dmitri relished every minute of it.

But others, like Cyril Magnin, who for years was considered the godfather of cultural activities in San Francisco, downplayed the importance of recognition.

Magnin's gifts to culture and the arts were substantial and regular. His largest gift houses a priceless jade collection in the Asian Art Wing of the M. H. deYoung Museum in San Francisco.

It's named in honor of his parents and his late wife, the only memorial that carries the Magnin name.

"The recognition of a gift means nothing to me, it makes no difference at all," Magnin told me. "I don't give for the sake of getting my name in the paper or for personal aggrandizement.

"The Magnin Jade Room was a major effort of

mine and I wanted to do something to recognize my parents and my wife." (Still, the casual observer would note that Magnin's name never failed to appear where he was a patron, whether the symphony, ballet, or a major museum.)

James Gamble, too, says accolades aren't important.

"I know a lot of people do like their names on the wall," he said. "But as far as I'm concerned, I don't feel recognition is necessary. All I want is some sort of an acknowledgement."

(I did notice, however, when visiting Gamble, there was a wall covered with certificates commemorating his gifts and board memberships.)

And then there's W. Clement Stone. He gave $1.5 million to a medical center in Korea. It was to honor a godly man who meant a great deal to Stone.

"They wanted to name the building after me," Stone said on the day I visited. "I told them I didn't want that, that's not what I had in mind.

"I gave the gift because of the vision of the priest who was so involved in the program. I told them to name the building after him," Stone said, as his secretary entered the office.

"I used to get quite upset about all of the fuss of recognition. But one day a wise man told me:

'Clem, you're very gracious in making your gifts. It's also wonderful to be gracious in receiving recognition.' So if the recognition comes, I accept it. But I never seek it."

On my way out, I took Stone's secretary aside and asked if this was really true. I had known Clem Stone for years and no one would describe him as the shrinking violet type. He was outgoing, dynamic, and his antennae were acutely attuned to the media.

"If he receives proper recognition, he accepts it," she told me. "If he doesn't get it, I honestly don't think it bothers him."

My experience with million dollar donors is that, most often, they don't care to ask for recognition but are grateful for the suggestion. From a fundraising standpoint, a proper celebration of the gift begets additional giving. From the donor and from others.

The donor may deny any desire for special recognition. He may hold his hand high in protest. But heed the experience of one of our country's major zoos.

When they somehow forgot to recognize their largest benefactor at the opening of their new addition – something the benefactor had made possible – you can bet the zoo sealed its future with respect to further gifts.

16

THOSE WHO GIVE, RECEIVE

"Charity is lending to the Lord, who in good times will return the gift with increase."

– Calvinist Reformers

I kept checking the address and the map as I drove to his office in Los Angeles. At best, this could be called a neighborhood in transition.

Security guards stood at the door of his headquarters, which was equipped with buzzers and one-way mirrors. A security guard accompanied me to his office, not a very fancy one for a man who had done so well.

I was visiting Gerald Jennings, the man who converted a baby carriage into the idea for a wheelchair. A crude model, but what a lifesaver. His wheelchair went on to become the Cadillac of the field, and the largest selling.

"It's a bewildering thing," he said to me. "When I first started in this business, we weren't making any money. We were just scratching out a living."

Nevertheless, Jennings and his wife decided to give away 10 percent of all they earned, meager as it was. "It was an easy decision. We weren't making any money. We wouldn't have much to give away."

It was just about this time, when the decision was made to tithe, that the business began to change. And the more it prospered, the more Jerry Jennings and his wife gave away.

There finally came a period when they were doing so well, there was barely time to keep up with it all. "It takes all the hours we have just to give it away," Jennings told me.

There is something bewildering about tithing. Mystifying. Even forgetting the biblical admonitions, it appears true – life is like a wheel, what you give comes right back to you.

Cotton Mather lived during the colonial era of this country and was one of its great philanthropists. He was instrumental in the founding of Yale University. He felt philanthropy was a matter of repaying God for the obligation that was owed. But he was also convinced that "those who devote themselves to good devices usually find a wonderful increase of their own opportunities."

Is it really possible? Can a case be made for philanthropy? I mean, can it be true that the more you give to charity, the more you receive in return? I don't mean personal joy or inner satisfaction. I am speaking of a direct monetary return.

O. V. Blumenstiel was an attorney in Alliance, Ohio. I was quite young in the business when he told me this story, but I remember it well.

His church, the First Presbyterian in Alliance, brought a small group of the leadership together to talk about tithing.

Vic said they were told that if they tithed, "they would be repaid many times over." What they gave would actually be given back to them – in multiples.

Vic was certain his minister was talking about the great satisfaction they would receive for the good they were doing.

"But a strange thing happened. I hate to even talk about it. I found that my tithing had an almost direct relationship to my law practice and what I received."

The more dollars he gave to charity, the greater his income. Not only did Vic have the satisfaction and inner joy of giving, but along with it he earned more.

I have heard it from many others. The same experience.

I don't suggest you tithe so you can earn more. Obviously, that would be the wrong reason. Grossly improper. But for some, perhaps that's reason enough.

Dortch Oldham made a decision to tithe before he graduated from college. He was working his way through school, supporting himself entirely. But a portion of his small earnings went regularly to the church.

He told me he had almost nothing. But no matter what he earned, a mite went to charity. As he prospered, he kept it up. He told me the more he gave, the more he seemed to have.

Some time ago I had dinner with Stuart Irby and his wife in their Jackson (Mississippi) home. Stuart was one of the community's most significant donors.

He had just that day made a gift of $2 million to French Camp Academy – one of his many passions. We were celebrating his gift over dinner.

I asked my question, as I always do when a

person makes a large gift.

"Stuart, do you find after you've made a large gift, the money somehow comes back to you?"

His wife said that was nonsense, impossible.

"Not so fast," said Stuart. "It's very strange. But every time I do make a sizable gift, the money does somehow comes back. And usually more."

When we were alone in his office, Alex Spanos confided the same thing to me.

Quietly he spoke. "The more I give, the more I make. I can't explain it, but I know it's true. I don't give for that reason. But it definitely seems to work out that way. It did from the very beginning when I really started to give."

There is a lesson here for fundraisers. But I don't know what it is or quite how to explain it.

I know we don't speak enough about the gospel of giving. How can we let people know there's often a direct return on their investment to charity? But at the same time, not put philanthropy on self-serving, quid pro quo terms.

Said Clement Stone, who gave away tens of millions in his lifetime. "I am absolutely certain – convinced – that the more I give away, the more I seem to receive in return."

It is clear. Those who give – receive in return. In multiples.

17

PASS IT ON

*"We must teach our children that what is ours in
life is only in trust, to be given to worthy causes –
and what man has in life he keeps only that which is
given away."*

– James Cash Penney

Common to all the mega givers I interviewed
is a compulsion to pass on to their children a
responsibility to give. This is the case even when
the donors were reared in families that were poor.

Alex Spanos has taught his offspring to be
philanthropic. "My children give," he says. "It's
one of the ways they say thanks to me. They know
when they give to a program that's important to
me, it makes me extremely happy. What else
would they give me? A tie? A book? Cufflinks?"

107

Spanos goes on to say his father knew nothing about giving. "It wasn't his fault. We were lucky to have enough to eat," he said.

"When you come from nothing as I did, you know what it's like to be poor. You understand better what a great joy it is to do something for others. If I can make others happy, if I can do good for others, that's a great satisfaction. I tried to help my children understand this feeling."

George Pardee had extraordinary success as a land developer and was identified with many important causes. "My mother and father were not givers," he said to me.

"As a matter of fact, they went bankrupt during the depression. I don't know what really has been the influence on me. I know a lot of my friends don't share the same concern for philanthropy I do, and I can't understand it."

Louise Davies clearly knew where her habit of giving came from. "Mother was always helping someone," she said. "We didn't have a lot of money or a lot of goods, but whatever there was she wanted to share it. I can still remember her saying, 'Hitch up the horse, we've got work to do.' And we'd be off and running to help a neighbor.

"My own children know how strongly I feel

about giving," Louise Davies told me. "I've tried to set a proper example. I can't do much more than that."

For those who were raised in well-to-do families, the responsibility to give, and to pass this heritage down, is perhaps even more ingrained.

Dorothy Simmerly comes from a family of tremendous financial resources. At one time, hers was one of the wealthiest families in the country. She says she was surrounded by giving and felt the responsibility from the very beginning.

"Mother was a giver and a very generous one. But she didn't talk to us directly about philanthropy. She didn't have to. The example she set was far more important than any words."

And I think of James N. Gamble, grandson of the founder of the Procter & Gamble Company, one of the world's leading suppliers of consumer goods. "I am a giver because of my upbringing," Gamble says. "There's no question about it."

Gamble speaks with special feeling about his father. "I remember when I was a teenager. Dad would sit down with me to talk about my D. B.'s – Deductible Benevolences.

"We didn't have a large allowance – Dad didn't want to spoil us. But he always stressed how we had the responsibility to use a certain percentage of whatever allowance there was for important causes. Dad would talk with us about this and help us in our thinking. This made a great impression on me. I do the same thing with my children today."

The Great Teacher said: Show me where a person puts his treasures and I'll show you where his heart is.

18

WHAT MEGA GIVERS EXPECT IN A FUNDRAISER

"When a person arrives in the world as a baby, his hands are clenched as though to say, 'Everything is mine, I will inherit it all.' When he departs from the world, his hands are open as though to say: 'I've acquired nothing from the world that I can keep for myself.'"

– Annie Dillard

I was talking with Malin Burnham the other day, chairman of one of southern California's oldest real estate firms (think 1891).

He had recently made a transformational gift to one of the most promising research centers in the nation. It's now called The Burnham Institute (La Jolla, California).

We were discussing what prompted his gift.

But more specifically, I wanted to know what qualities he admired most in a fundraiser, someone calling on him for a gift.

Believe me, he's had plenty of folks calling on him. And he's been extremely generous. When I asked the question, he didn't hesitate for a moment.

"There needs to be a near-militant belief in its mission," he tells me. "When someone calls on me, I can tell if there's a passion for the organization. I can actually feel it. If the fundraiser isn't deeply committed, how can they expect me to be?"

Malin also expects a high level of energy. Just a few days before, a solicitor had called on him. "She was absolutely charged," he says. "As she spoke about her project, there was electricity in the air. I couldn't help but feel the glow."

I could tell Malin was warming up to the subject. "I'll tell you a quality I don't like. Someone calling on me who's pushy. I dig in my feet. Or someone who never stops talking. How are they ever going to know what *I'm* interested in?"

Malin leaves until last what he considers the most important attribute of a successful fundraiser.

"Nothing is more important than integrity,"

he says. "I look for it every time someone calls on me. If it's not there, I can spot it immediately."

I agree with Malin. I consider integrity the mightiest weapon in a fundraiser's arsenal. More important than any other single quality. Its power is explosive. Integrity alone won't get you a ticket to the top, but without it, you can't even begin the journey.

There are some other attributes beyond what Malin Burnham talked to me about.

For one thing, I find the great fundraisers are much like folks who pull up the roots to see if the flowers are still growing! They are *itchy* by nature. They don't easily suffer standing still or treading water. Status quo is anathema to them.

I'm reminded that every morning in Africa, a gazelle wakes up. It knows it must run faster than the lion or it will be eaten. Every morning a lion wakes up. It knows it must outrun the slowest gazelle or it will starve to death.

It doesn't matter whether you're the lion or the gazelle – when the sun comes up, you'd better be running. The great fundraiser understands this.

Oh, there's lots more. Self-confidence. Comfort in one's own skin. Genuine affection for people. Authenticity.

But let me finish with a characteristic I find in all of the great fundraisers: They love their work.

There is a willingness to pay the price – whatever the cost. Their work becomes something of an obsession. It burns like fire in their bones.

You've heard the dictum: No pain, no gain. Success in raising money is a moving target. Often, a fundraiser can feel a bit like Odysseus, the hero of Homer's *Odyssey* – "My life is endless trouble and chaos."

There are the long hours, long days, some of which seem never to end. But still there is joy and exhilaration, fulfillment and an inner glow.

When you think about it, the reason is obvious. Fundraising has the power to dramatically impact society in a way no other profession can. And you're an integral part of that noble pursuit.

John R. Mott, one of the great Christian voices of the mid-1900s, was right. He said: "Blessed are the fundraisers, and in heaven they shall stand on the right hand of the martyrs."

19

YOUR BEST APPROACH

"The greatest and highest level of giving is the
person who gives without knowing to whom the gift
is made, and the recipient does not know from whom
he receives. And it matters not who makes the
request for the gift or how it is made. The joyful and
true giver cares not."

– Maimonides

Dr. Vartan Gregorian heads the Carnegie Corporation. He now gives away money instead of
asking for it. (For many, that would be like the
refrain from a popular song in *My Fair Lady*:
"That's my idea of heavenly heaven.")

When I asked Gregorian about his well-known
fundraising prowess, he denied it vehemently.
And not out of modesty (which isn't one of

Vartan's principal virtues).

"As president of Brown University, I raised a great deal of money. And before that as president of the New York Public Library. But as a matter of fact, I've never asked anyone for a gift. Not ever."

Dear reader, I see your quizzical face. But keep reading.

"I let them know about my dreams and vision for the future," continues Gregorian. "I explain how important the program is and about the lives it affects.

"When I finish, it seems I never have to ask. They always come forward with what they want to do. It has become their dream and vision."

Gregorian makes it sound simple. But this doesn't give credit to the impact he has on a person when describing his bold and exciting dreams. Vartan Gregorian is magic.

The late Edmund L. Keeney, M.D., who directed the Scripps Clinic (La Jolla, California) never asked for money either. Yet he was one of the most successful fundraisers in Southern California.

When Keeney visited with a prospect, he walked them through the new medical library, he rhapsodized about the advances a new cancer research center could make, he extolled the life-saving possibilities of a new surgical suite. Before long, the prospect became part of Keeney's exciting and provocative vision.

Keeney always talked about "something" but he never talked about money. He sold the dream, and did it with such conviction and persuasiveness it was impossible to resist.

Both Gregorian and Keeney instinctively understood mega givers. They knew that dreams and visions and possibilities were the way to their heart.

Jim Gamble confirms this. "I get so tired of it," he tells me. "People come in and talk and talk. And all they talk about is the three Bs – Buildings, Benefactors, and Baloney."

Tell me about the dream, is what Gamble is saying.

Underline this next sentence. For your prospects, giving is about changing lives and saving lives. It's not about the money.

"All I want to do is to save the world," says Marianne McDonald.

Your donors may be less global than Marianne but the intent is the same. They want their gift to make a difference. Your job is to describe how your institution can make that difference in a way uniquely its own.

And if you want to stoke the desire of mega givers, it had better be a pressing *human* need you're trying to meet. (If it has emotional appeal and makes the hair on the back of the neck stand up, all the better.)

"I need to hear the problem is urgent," Clement Stone told me, "something that needs to be solved immediately. And if it's exciting and makes me tingle, the institution is well on its way to getting my gift."

The mega donors went on to say more. They want the case for the project presented in a persuasive and dramatic way, but devoid of small details. And the actual presentation shouldn't take too long – perhaps seven or eight minutes.

"No fluff," is the way Marianne McDonald put it. "I want to hear a quick, sound rationale regarding the project and its validity."

Another point these donors make is that any attempt to be pushy and heavy-handed is a turn-off. McDonald is clear about this.

"I don't like people who tell me what I must or should do. I resist that kind of approach," she said with some vehemence.

Every mega giver is unique. Each has idiosyn-cracies. And their own dreams. Each will be stirred in different ways.

This explains why it's critical to know your prospect before actually asking for the gift. This often requires research and perhaps several vis-its.

Still, if I am to boil it down to the one approach that consistently works with mega givers, I admonish: Listen. Listen intently. Listen even more intently. Sell the dream, not the project. And tell how lives will be changed.

Will this work with your donors? I leave you with the wisdom of Dr. Seuss (*Oh, the Places You'll Go!*):

"And will you succeed?
Yes! Yes! You will indeed!
(98 and 1/4 percent guaranteed.)"

20

THE JOY OF GIVING

"God loveth a cheerful giver."

– St. Paul
In his Second Letter to the
Congregation at Corinth

I saved the best for last.

The issue was never really raised. Yet, it was a persistent theme dominating nearly every interview. It was true with every single donor. It dealt with the joy of giving, the sheer ecstasy.

I reviewed with each person the factors that motivated their giving. A recurring pattern was the towering gratification they received from making the gift.

I never initiated this aspect of the discussion. The comments flowed freely from each individual.

Louise M. Davies talked to me about the joy of her giving. "When Ralph and I first started out, he was earning $300 a month," she said. "But even then, he was giving to special projects."

When Ralph died, the janitor from the company walked up to Louise and held her hand. "Mr. Davies put all of my seven children through school and college," he told her. "Without him, it couldn't have happened."

Louise had no idea.

"As time went on, I found out more about the small things he had done. I think he gave for the sheer joy of giving. I know I do."

Cyril Magnin knew the feeling. "I love to give," he told me. "It gives me great joy and satisfaction. I want to be here to see people enjoy it. That means a great deal to me."

For the donor, giving does something almost indescribable. Let me tell you about William Black, founder of Chock Full O' Nuts coffee.

In the early 1930s, Black converted his chain of nut shops into stores that sold a sandwich and a cup of coffee for a nickel. In its heyday, there were over 100 Chock Full O' Nuts coffee shops in and around New York City.

Black gave away millions to New York medical schools and hospitals. He described the feeling eloquently.

"Wouldn't you be thrilled to feel financially responsible, partly or wholly, for a major breakthrough against a dread disease? I'm thrilled to see my name inscribed in a plaque at the Columbia University Medical Research Center. Who wouldn't be?"

Black went on. "Doesn't the author feel joy in seeing his book in the bookstore window? Doesn't the artist sign his painting out of a feeling of accomplishment? I, too, am quietly happy and deeply grateful I've been able to contribute something to society. It gives me immense joy."

It has been my experience, confirmed by every one of my mega givers, that there's a satisfaction to giving that knows no bounds.

By and large, giving isn't done to challenge others, or to meet averages, or percentages. These are factors, all important but peripheral. Joy – that is the inner motivation.

Annabelle and Bernard Fishman, of Philadelphia, give for the sheer joy of it. They made their money in real estate and investments. For their 25th wedding anniversary, the couple decided to build a school in Jerusalem.

There was no direct connection, no ties to the children or the school principal. The Fishmans just felt it would be a fun thing to do. And tremendously important, too.

When the school was dedicated, the Fishmans and their family went to Jerusalem for the ceremony. It was a touching experience. And a tremendous moment. In fact, it was so joyous that on their visit they gave another $2 million to endow the school.

George Pardee understood the joy. "The truth of the matter is that I'm terribly happy to be in a position where I can make large gifts," he told me. "I think people who are generous givers tend to be happy people. Part of it comes from the fact that it's so much fun to be able to give."

There really is something to that. I have thought a lot about Pardee's comment that givers are happy people. It's true.

Among all I interviewed, there was an inner glow, a sense of great happiness. And a transcendent attitude about their achievements in life and about their giving. You feel it. You can almost touch it. This has been true, also, throughout my experience in the field.

It's a gross generalization to say so, but I find

most major donors are cheerful, positive people. Pleased with themselves. Their station in life. Happy to be in a position to be making a gift.

For some, making a gift of real consequence to an institution may be like "hitting the wall" in a marathon. It is painful at first, then it begins feeling good. In the end it's euphoric.

"My God, I've done it!" said Marianne McDonald after making her first *hitting the wall* gift. That's when it first occurred to me that a "gloomy giver" is an oxymoron.

McDonald told me about a gift-naming contribution she made to honor her brother. The day she made the gift, she was so excited she couldn't sleep a wink that evening. Not a wink.

When she got out of bed the next morning, she went to her bathroom, turned on the light, and looked in the mirror. She spread her arms well above her head and cried out: "Marianne, you are one hell of a lady."

Not often in a person's lifetime is there an opportunity to do something significant, something really consequential. Something of lasting value.

Giving to a really great cause isn't a duty. It is a joy. One that we too seldom sell or communicate to the donor.

21

TENETS FOR SUCCESS

"He who is inclined to making many learned pro-
nouncements and practicing profundity, is in grave
danger of being compared to the black-smith's bel-
lows— providing great bursts of hot air under pressure, but having not spark nor fire in itself."

— John Lewis Russell

What does it all mean?

I spoke with more than 50 men and women
who had made gifts of $1 million or more. I also
collected data from more than a thousand
fundraising professionals.

As for me, I bring over 40 years to this magnificent business of helping others undertake consequential acts of kindness and generosity.

What I have discovered is that there are clearly

127

factors and forces that motivate large gifts.

The proof is irrefutable. There is more commonality in the factors than there are differences. And as extraordinarily unique as people are, the drive and consideration that propels them to a major gift is very much the same.

During the preparation of this book I combined all I heard from my donors and all I could read on the subject. I mixed this generously and openly with my own feelings and attitudes.

What has evolved are 62 factors that I am convinced guide, shape, and determine the success of securing the mega gifts. Here they are.

1   Don't say 'no' for anyone.

Be bold and daring. Go after your top prospects with persistence and passion, and all the vigor and zeal you can muster. You'll be hurt more by those who would have said "yes," but weren't asked, than by those who say "no."

Few commandments in fundraising are as sacrosanct as this. Note it well.

2   Giving by living men and women outstrips every other form of philanthropy.

Over 80¢ of every dollar is given by a living man or woman. This has been true for the last 20 years. Another 10¢ comes from estates. The result is that 90 percent of all giving comes from individuals, not foundations and corporations.

This highlights the importance of developing a creative strategy for the weighing, wooing, and winning of your individual prospects.

Obviously, keep in mind that corporate boards, and foundation executives, consist of people with the same blend of human strengths and frailties, agonies and joys, that guide the giving of individuals.

A foundation may have well defined roles that govern its funding, but even within these limitations, the foundation executive and board will often make decisions with the same intuitions, perceptions, and feelings as individuals.

3 **Individuals give emotionally, not cerebrally.**

Men and women don't give to needs. They give to dreams and dazzling visions.

Giving is visceral. Individuals will view your long list of details and specifics with pious and quiet admiration, but this will seldom move mega givers to audacious action.

The best auto salesman gets you into the driver's seat. You feel the wheel. You look at the gleaming dashboard. For one glorious moment, you're speeding through the Italian Alps.

For most people, reading the torque-ratios and compression factors may be interesting, but it's the driver's seat that moves them. Get your prospect behind the steering wheel and in the driver's seat!

Walk the prospect through the campus or into the emergency room of the hospital. Help them remember what it was like to be nine years old and away at camp.

4   The 'Rule of Thirds' is a canon that has persisted since the earliest of fundraising programs.

It persists today and while there may be some exceptions, the Rule is virtually scriptural: one-third of your funds in a campaign will come from your top 10 to 15 gifts; one-third will come from your next 100 to 125 gifts; the remaining one-third will come from all the other gifts.

There is evidence that larger gifts are more important than ever. Now we find that about 95 percent of the funds come from three to four percent of the donors. The base of the giving pyramid is less broad. The tip, more crucial than ever.

And don't think you can discard the Rule of Thirds with egalitarian giving. It has been attempted often, and always with disastrous results. The project is moribund.

A Midwestern college needs to quickly raise $600,000 to finance a project. "That should be easy," says one enthusiastic alumnus. "We'll just get 600 of our graduates to give $1,000 each."

Never! It simply won't work. The Rule of Thirds will prevail – $200,000 will come from the top 10 to 15 gifts. The same Rule applies to a $6 million, or a $66 million campaign.

5   **Virtually without exception, husbands and wives (and partners) discuss their major philanthropy.**

Husbands and wives will confer before making a final commitment for a mega gift. You can count on it. So give serious thought to initiating your discussion about the gift with

131

both the husband and wife, even though only one partner may be especially interested in your program.

Otherwise, you risk having the whole discussion about giving take place without your being present to run interference, respond to questions, and overcome objections.

6   **Seek ways to involve both the husband and the wife in the program and activities of the institution.**

Make certain both receive credit and recognition, even if only one partner carried the major responsibility for the gift. This lessens the possibility of divided loyalties. And it helps ensure a continued interest in your institution by the surviving spouse.

7   **There's no clear evidence the spirit, passion, and dedication to philanthropy is passed to the next generation.**

Countless examples confirm this (though you will find many notable exceptions).

If you go after the son or daughter for a gift because the parent was extremely generous, it is entirely possible you'll be on a misguided, misdirected mission. The new generation will have its own unique desires and passions.

8   **It is harder to get an appointment than it is to secure the gift.**

More intensive planning and innovation may be required to get the appointment than is needed to sell the program. Develop a strategy for securing the visit. It's every bit as important as your plan for getting the gift.

Use the best person and contact possible to make the appointment and open the door. Always remember: getting the appointment is 85 percent of getting the gift.

9   **A good friend often isn't the best person to solicit the gift – although he or she may be the best to make the appointment.**

Often, a friend will be overly protective and may find it hard to overcome a negative attitude on the part of the potential donor. Instead of asking for a gift, it will be much easier for the friend to switch to making a date for next week's golf match.

There is another problem as well. A friend

often feels that asking for a gift can damage the relationship.

Secure the appointment with the help of a friend, and send someone with the friend who can ask for the gift.

10 In my experience, children aren't effective in soliciting their parents for a major gift.

Without question, they will be effective in securing gifts for a pet project, but seldom a mega gift. I have questioned a number of professionals in the field on this subject, and I find total agreement.

Nonetheless, children can be very helpful in encouraging and supporting the parent's decision to make the gift.

An interesting twist. I've had a number of couples ask that their gift be anonymous. They didn't want their children to know about it!

11 Securing the mega gift means helping the donor share your dream.

Your objective must fit the donor's design and interest. The sooner your vision is shared and becomes the donor's dream and passion, the quicker the decision will be to give.

Successful fundraising is helping others to meet their needs while accomplishing yours.

12 The decision to give is spontaneous.

There's almost an immediate spark of electricity. The amount may still be in doubt, the timing may be a question, the manner in which the gift will finally be made may require further study – but the decision is made. A strike of lightning!

If the potential donor requests a great deal of time to make a decision or, if on subsequent visits, no definite move puts the gift into action, the odds are you're not going to receive a significant gift.

13 The commitment regarding the major gift will likely not be made on the first visit.

If it is, there's a good possibility you're leaving money on the table.

The reason we call a large sum *a stop-and-think-gift* is because the stretch gift requires time to come to a resolution.

This being the case, spend most of your time during the first call selling the drama, the power, and the excitement of the program.

14 The case for the gift must be stronger and bigger than the institution itself.

You must demonstrate a broader platform than just the institution. Examine how the project reaches far beyond the institution itself – to the community, to the nation, to the world.

15 Don't sell the needs of the institution.

Virtually all organizations need money. But people don't give to needs. They give to opportunities. Bold, visionary, exhilarating opportunities.

Donors require their own needs to be met. Listen carefully. See how you can mold the needs of the potential donor to the opportunities of the proposed program.

Mega givers will buy what they choose, not what you're trying to sell. The trick is in making certain what they want most is what you want most.

When Robert Schuller decided he needed to expand his church to meet a bulging membership of 8000, every addition and renovation the architect proposed met with a dull, uninspired ho-hum by his board of directors.

Then a visionary Schuller said: "I want a totally new church, all glass. All glass!" Now that was an audacious opportunity.

He inspired his congregation to make his dream theirs. What evolved is the Crystal Cathedral. All glass, star shaped, 414 feet from one point to the other. The glass roof is one hundred feet longer than a football field and seems to float in space. It soars 12 stories above the ground.

16 Listen.

The more you listen, the more you learn. Probe and ask questions. If you listen carefully, you'll know precisely what interests the prospect.

17 Listen!

18 Mega givers are filled with joy.

You can pick them out in a crowd. I haven't been able to figure out why, but it's true – there's a sparkle and recognizable joy to their living – a *joie de vivre*.

It may be they've reached the stage where they're now able to make a large gift – reason enough for joy. It may be that because they make large gifts, they feel they're on the right side of the angels. Whatever it is, there is the definite thrill and joy of living.

My eyes tell me mega givers live beyond the actuarial tables. Gerontologists claim that people live longer when there is the will and the drive to live, and the joy of the moment, the hope for the future. Perhaps this is the connection.

You doubt me. Just think of the really large donors you know. Note their age and attitude. Then write me a letter of apology.

19 A person with no experience in giving will very rarely make a major first gift.

Giving is a habit. The fact that a person has great resources offers no assurance that a gift will be made. I'm talking about a large gift.

How often have you heard: "She has enough money to fund the whole campaign." But she won't, not if she hasn't had the experience and exhilaration of giving in the past. It's like getting the first olive out of the jar.

Make the call anyway. You can't win if you

don't begin. Be satisfied with a smaller gift than you had hoped for. Show appreciation, cultivate, recognize. Call again for a gift. And again.

Gradually, that smaller first gift will grow into a much larger one.

20 Believe.

Feel and think what it will be like to secure the mega gift. Engage the extraordinary power of the possible. Make a giant leap of faith. If you're fairly certain you won't get a gift, the odds are you won't.

21 Major donors give their largest gift to those institutions where they serve on the board or in a volunteer capacity.

It's a plain fact that familiarity begets involvement, and involvement begets commitment, and commitment begets giving. Often, sacrificial giving.

The more people know about you and the more involved they are, the more likely they are to be committed to your great aspirations and grand designs. Involvement provides a quantum escalation to a mega gift.

It doesn't necessarily follow that everyone on the board will make a stretch gift. But you'll find your most sacrificial gifts do come from people on the board or those who have served in some official capacity in the past.

22 Dedicated, devoted board members are the lifeblood of an organization.

The strong, effective, influential, and affluential men and women – the four "W" variety – are becoming increasingly difficult to recruit. Your board profile provides one of the vital signs of the organization's health, an unshakable index of your ability and vitality to grow and develop.

Potential board members who show promise and resolve should be pursued and romanced with the same ardor you place in engineering a large gift. These dedicated 4-W board members are a treasure to be coveted.

A board of dogged determination and dedication can accomplish any objective for your institution.

23 Mega givers feel a sense of duty and responsibility in their giving.

Among those who give, there is a deep sense of gratitude.

Life has been strikingly good to them. There is the compulsion to repay somehow for this good fortune.

The mega givers are asked often. There's no end to the number of requests. One after another. But they keep giving.

At times, they must feel like the man who in desperation calls an angel for some relief from the barrage of solicitations. The angel appears.

"Angel, angel – how long must
I keep giving?"
The angel looked at the man –
The glance pierced him through.
"You may stop giving,
When the Lord stops giving to you."

Mega givers don't give out of a sense of guilt. Definitely not. But for some, their may be a slight nod to voodoo and the supernatural. Just in case!

24 Staff leadership determines the character, the vitality, the growth, and the personality of an institution.

A dynamic institution is led by a dynamic staff. Propelled with the zeal of a fervent missionary.

Mega givers respond to vigorous and inspirational staff leadership. It is one of the most compelling factors in motivating their gift.

In all my experience, I don't know of a really major gift made to an institution where the donor didn't have high regard and respect for the Chief Executive Officer.

Take the following as gospel. No matter how dedicated the Christian is to his church, he will give even more if he has steadfast admiration for the minister.

No matter how grateful a person is to the hospital, she will give an even greater amount if she has esteem for the staff.

No matter how sentimental a man may feel about his alma mater, the gift will be even more sacrificial if there's affection and admiration for the President.

I know of no situation to challenge this

hypothesis. The consequential role staff plays in motivating the mega gift is irrefutable.

25 The staff is singularly dominant in motivating the mega gift – particularly the Chief Executive Officer.

It is critical to have the Chief Executive Officer involved in some significant way in developing the solicitation strategy and actually making the call for a large gift. It pays proper respect to the donor and is immensely effective in influencing the gift.

For the solicitation, have the CEO make the call with a high ranking volunteer – and you have a *Magic Partnership*.

26 Chief Executive Officers who do well at fundraising enjoy it.

Some thrive on it. A few even lust for it. Those who don't do well, don't like it.

27 For a successful solicitation, a volunteer must be head-over-heels devoted to the cause.

With regard to volunteers soliciting large donors, it's far better to have a lower level volunteer with a passionate commitment than a higher level volunteer who is a lukewarm advocate.

In other words, the most influential person won't necessarily be your most effective solicitor unless he or she brings an immovable, overwhelming, uncompromising commitment to the program. Passion on fire!

And, of course, the volunteer must have made her own gift before making the call. A stretch gift.

28 Determine with painstaking strategy who should make the call.

Generalizations are seldom valid. I know that. I live by that. And I never forget fundraising is more art than science. But here are some principles you can count on (most of the time! – which is the price you pay for generalizing).

It is difficult for a younger woman to solicit an older woman or widow. The latter is accustomed to dealing with older attorneys and accountants, most often her husband's and most often male. She is comfortable in this setting, much less so with the young female.

Nuns are more effective when they wear their habit. They can be persuasive calling on both men and women. Priests, on the other hand, are more effective calling on women.

As mentioned earlier, sons and daughters aren't effective in securing major gifts from their parents. But a parent can be extremely successful in soliciting one of the children.

29 Mega givers experience a spiritual sensation in their giving.

This doesn't necessarily have anything to do with the formal church or organized religion. But there is the touch and tingle of righteousness, sometimes even close to piousness, in the giving of mega donors.

There is almost always a great deal of affection and near reverence for the institution that is the beneficiary of the mega gift.

For many, when the gift is made, there is a mystical soul-stirring which transcends the commonplace. It is an important factor in motivating the large giver. Not God-fearing, but godly.

145

30 **Never in American history has there been an era with greater urgency for the delivery of human and social services.**

It is a time of clatter and clang. Emergencies and exigencies. Clamor and crunch.

There is an explosive precedence for services – balanced unevenly by reductions in federal and state funds. Add to that the sobering reduction in corporate and foundation giving, and what you have is an unrelenting burden on the private sector for financing.

That's good news! Well, yes! Good news. As Clement Stone was so fond of saying: "You have a problem – that's great!"

Problems represent swelling expectations and magnificent opportunities. Donors are just waiting for bold and daring institutions sufficiently venturesome to reach out.

There's no lack of money, only a lack of vision. It's there, all yours, for the asking.

31 **Recognition of the donor is important – expressing appropriate appreciation, even more so.**

While most mega givers don't seek undue

recognition, I am convinced that appropriate honor, tastefully and tactfully rendered, is welcomed and appreciated.

Don't expect the donor to ask or seek this type of singling out (though some will!). You must initiate the idea, encourage it, and review it with the individual.

The dividends for carefully planning and developing such visible appreciation will be immense. And it initiates the first step in securing another and larger gift.

32 Quite often, a donor doesn't wish public tribute for making a mega gift.

Still, it is extremely important to your institution that recognition be given for the gift. It paves the way for gifts to follow. Suggest a way to honor the donor's family, a loved one, or a tribute to someone he or she greatly admires.

The gift needn't pay tribute to the actual donor. The glow can be just as bright when a family member or loved one is honored.

When it was suggested to Marianne McDonald that the proposed Alcohol Treatment Center be named for the deceased brother she adored, the idea of the gift was sealed. He had died of an overdose!

At the Asheville School (North Carolina) a couple wanted to name a building for their son who died in an auto accident. But they had a daughter in her junior year at the school.

They were rightfully concerned about naming the building while their daughter was still at school. We suggested they make the gift (anonymously) on the stipulation the building be named two years hence after she graduated.

Probe, explore, plumb the possibilities.

33 Practice the 'Rule of Sevens.'

Find a way to thank a person seven times for their gift. I don't believe in formula-guaranteed answers to fundraising. But this one really works. I promise. The results will astound you.

I view all forms of appreciation and recognition as a sacrament, a kind of holy water, to be splattered on at every opportunity with the largest possible aspergill.

34 Asking for a mega gift during lunch or dinner isn't encouraged.

Find a quiet place (often in the donor's environment or where the donor is most at ease) and you won't be disturbed at the crucial moment of asking for the gift ("Would anyone care for coffee?").

35 Large donors tend to stay with programs and activities that have been of interest over a long time.

Major donors don't bounce from one institution to another. If you're calling on a prospective donor, one who has been a major donor to other institutions but hasn't given yet to yours, the chances are slim you will receive a mega gift the first time around.

But it's certainly worth the attempt. Go after the prospect with all of the faith and hope you can marshal. Use the most powerful ammunition you can fire.

Almost certainly, you'll get a gift. It may not be as large as you wanted, but it will be a start.

Build on that. Celebrate the gift. Shower appreciation. Keep calling. Keep asking for new gifts and upgrading. That's the road to a mega gift.

36 **Exciting and daring programs sell.**

Mega donors are interested in programs that are significant and can make a difference. Bold, but conventional. Controversial and radical programs are often extremely difficult to sell – no matter how great the urgency and need.

37 **Those who will give to you in the future are men and women who have given to you in the past.**

Your best prospects for a gift are those who have already given to you.

This tenet is flawless, even if a sizable gift has just been made to your institution. Say, for instance, you're very near the completion of your campaign – the bottom half of the ninth inning! But you still haven't reached your goal.

You evaluate the prospects who still haven't committed to the program. You make a careful examination. The appraisal looks promising, but it still doesn't appear you'll be able to reach your goal.

What to do? Should you call on those who

have already given to the campaign – but haven't done as much as they could have or you expected? No! Don't call on them.

Instead, call on those who have already made a very large and generous gift. They will do more. And they will be pleased you asked.

38 **No matter how exciting and tantalizing the program, donors are less likely to give to an institution with financial problems.**

Financial stability of the institution is considered one of the prime requisites of the donor. No one wants to give to save the sinking Titanic.

There's little comfort in making a mega gift unless there is assurance and confidence the organization has had a sound fiscal operation in the past and shows financial promise for the future.

This need not be the major emphasis in a presentation – after all, this is not selling "the sizzle." On the other hand, proper fiduciary responsibility and stewardship do need to be stressed.

39 People don't give from a sense of guilt.

They don't give "till it hurts." They give because it feels exhilirating. The spirit soars.

There's no guilt. Donors are thrilled to be in a position to give.

40 Ego plays an important part in making a mega gift.

Most of the men and women who make large gifts concede there's a tremendous amount of ego involved in their philanthropy. The recognition, the status it provides, the acclaim, and for some the permanent memorializing of their name.

Even among those who vehemently deny any narcissistic factor to their philanthropy, I find a certain degree of self-serving indulgence. Not necessarily bluster, vain adulation, or aggrandizement. Still, an unquestionable self-satisfaction and self-regard.

Even under protest, tickle the ego!

41 A compelling, driving belief in the organization is singularly important.

A love of the organization takes precedence over local pride and community spirit. Mega gifts are indeed made because the donor feels the particular program will be good for the community, but overriding that issue is a passion for the overall organization.

First sell the institution, then interpret how the program can be of everlasting benefit to the community, or to the world.

42 Donors want to give to a cause of consequential proportions, a program with the potential for creating a significant change for good.

Before making the call on the potential donor, review carefully your presentation. Determine how the project can be developed into one which creates substantial, innovative, and positive outcomes.

Even a new roof should be transformed into a selling point of significance – as long as it can be shown to be a reordering of social and human services.

The new roof is the steak. Serving mankind under that roof is the sizzle.

43 Take nothing for granted.

Even members of the official institutional family, your closest board members, may not be as aware as you assume of your activities, your services, and your outreach.

You sit and wonder how someone who has served on your board for years may still not tingle with the excitement of your program.

Take my word for it, many do not. Even with those closest to you, take the time to impart the full drama of your story.

44 Donors are intrigued by the yeast, not the pabulum.

"Seed gifts" have great appeal. Show donors how their contribution can multiply gifts from countless others. This demonstrates that their dollars generate additional dollars in geometric proportions.

There's something else. In our campaigns, I tell our board and major donors that early gifts are the very best and most important. They have a multiplying impact and establish the pattern for gifts that follow.

I admonish my campaign workers to remember EMILY: Early Money Is Like Yeast.

45 Men and women give to institutions, programs, and campaigns that are successful.

They give to programs that are popular. Programs subscribed to by others. They race for the bandwagon. They disdain the losing cause, the unpopular program, the campaign that is faltering.

Success succeeds. The successful institution becomes more successful. The organization that needs help the most is likely to be overlooked.

46 Mega gifts are almost certain to be repeated.

Your best and largest donors are those who have given to you in the past. And rarely will their most recent gift be their largest or their last.

47 People resent overbearing solicitors.

They resist pressure and find it acutely

155

repugnant. The most effective solicitor listens – and then moves directly to make the potential donor's dream one and the same with that of the institution.

48 Who makes the call for a gift is of critical importance, but it does not have to be a peer.

Being a peer can be important for opening the door, making the appointment, and being present for the solicitation. A peer may not, however, be the best person possible for interpreting the institution or actually asking for the gift.

The hoary myth of peer calling on peer can often be a downright mistake.

49 Mega givers refer to one quality in particular they feel is most important in the person making the call: integrity.

They must respect the person and hold him or her in high regard and esteem. This is true whether the solicitor is a staff person or a volunteer.

As far as a staff person is concerned, the mega givers list integrity first. Then they talk about the 3 Es. What they like to see in the staff person is Energy, Enthusiasm, and Empathy.

50 Matching the gift of others has little effect in motivating mega givers.

Matching gifts don't motivate mega givers. However, being asked to make a *challenge* gift will often inspire them to reach higher.

51 For many, campaign literature creates the same boom as the sound of one hand clapping.

Often, campaign material is a turn-off. A negative. And the fancier the material, the more objectionable it is to donors.

The majority of serious donors much prefer a strong and compelling oral presentation, substantiated by simple written documentation.

Campaign literature can help influence smaller and medium sized gifts. It can also provide aid and comfort to the solicitor.

But for the really large size gift, use a different approach. Try the three-ring binder, replete with enticing photographs. Nothing is more effective.

52 More than two people can make an effective call.

A fundraising tale, repeated so often it is now accepted as Grail, says that more than two people making the solicitation are overwhelming to the prospective donor.

Not true!

Take as many people as you need. No fewer, no more. Just make certain you have a role for each.

53 Research your prospect with finite care and painstaking attention.

No detail is too small. What might appear to be an insignificant bit of information can often open the door to the mega gift.

54 Give your case a cold and calculating examination.

You may find it isn't a compelling and winning case at all. It may not have drama and emotional appeal. It may not provide the sizzle. The urgency.

There have been many instances where a small twist, a seemingly unimportant change, has made all the difference.

Take for instance the campaign for the Restoration of the Presidential Yacht Potomac. Funds were required to restore the Yacht. It was lifted from the sea floor, rescued from the salt water by a miracle of engineering and cranes, and completely stripped.

But the Potomac has little value as a vessel. It wasn't the first of its kind or the only one of its kind. Its fascination lies in the fact that during some of the most crucial years in the history of this nation, it was "the floating White House." It is where Franklin D. Roosevelt held many important meetings.

The restoration of the Yacht had little appeal, until the case for the campaign focused on President Roosevelt and the historic magic of the Presidency.

55 The mission of the organization is of primary, overriding, and paramount significance.

Nothing else is as important. Everything else pales in comparison. No matter how appealing the specific program or project may seem, nothing is as powerful an incentive as an abiding and unalterable belief in the mission of the institution.

Don't discuss the program, the campaign, the need. First, sell the mission.

56 Major gifts are made to change lives or save lives.

It is now quite clear men and women give because they feel they are making a difference. Marianne McDonald says all she wants to do is to change the world. She feels she can help achieve this through her giving.

The foremost reason mega donors give is to change lives or save lives. And they feel, because of your singular mission, this can be most effectively achieved through your organization.

Whatever your program or project, demonstrate how it will change and save lives. That gets to the inspirational and motivating kernel of the gift.

57 The more donors give, the more they get back.

This is a fascinating, almost mystical, by-product to philanthropy. Givers receive in return many-fold what they give away.

Giving is like a moving wheel. The more you give, the more you get back.

This cannot be explained, but it is recognized by major donors. It's not the reason they give, nor the motivating factor, nor the rationale. But the phenomenon does exist.

58 Individuals tend to be less conforming in their bequests, but more conservative in their giving while living.

The majority of mega givers live prudent and conventional lives. They prefer a similar pattern for their philanthropy while they are alive.

59 There is seldom a single, dominant reason for making a mega gift.

Most often, the mega gift is the result of several motivating factors. Often, these aren't understood or recognized even by the donor. And often they intersect and overlap.

When visiting the potential donor, explore, probe, and listen. Then, appeal to what you feel are the most stirring and provoking motivations.

60 The mega giver takes every advantage of the tax laws. But tax savings isn't the primary force behind giving.

And for many, tax isn't a factor at all. Don't sell the tax advantage. Don't even assume it will have an impact on the donor's giving to your program.

Place the strength and power of your presentation on the mission of your institution – and how it is uniquely positioned to change or save lives.

61 Fundraisers must consistently and persistently seek out the potential mega giver.

Fundraisers can be characterized by what William James calls "the faithful fighters." It's what the Greeks called the *Agon* – the struggle, the match. (It is also the derivative for the word agony!)

Fundraisers are an unusual lot. They love the battle and the struggle. Every day, they roll their rock up the hill. They enjoy the exhilaration of the fray. The strategy. The winning.

When the tardy and reluctant Crillon arrived too late for a great victory, Henry IV said: "Hang yourself, brave Crillon! We fought at Arques and you were not there."

To be an effective fundraiser requires a quality of intrepidity, persistence, and timing. For the fundraiser who has surrendered a mega gift to another institution: hang yourself – the precious moment existed, and you were not there.

Next time, seize the opportunity.

62 Many tenets are important, but the greatest of all is: You must ask for the gift.

This may appear overly fundamental but too often this cardinal principle is overlooked.

Many superb presentations are made where the interpretation and story of the institution are flawless, but where the solicitor finds it agonizing to ask for the gift. The tongue gets heavy and thick, the hands perspire.

But every salesperson knows that finally, inevitably – you must ask for the order. Ask for the gift. This is the greatest commandment of all.

It's absolutely amazing what you don't get when you don't ask!

About the Author

In *Born to Raise*, the author wrote: "Someone once told me that my career would have five stages: 1) Who is Jerry Panas? 2) Get me Jerry Panas, 3) We need someone like Jerry Panas, 4) What we need is a young Jerry Panas, and 5) Who is Jerry Panas?"

Jerry believes he's somewhere between stages two and three. "But," he says, "my friends indicate I'm somewhere in stage four, quickly approaching stage five!"

Hailed in Newsweek as "the Robert Schuller of fundraising," Jerry is the author of nine books, many of them classics in the field. He's also a popular columnist for *Contributions* magazine and a familiar and favorite speaker at conferences and workshops throughout the nation.

A senior officer of one of America's premier fundraising firms, Jerry lives with his wife, Felicity, in a 1710 Farmhouse in northwest Connecticut.

INDEX

The Gold Standard in Books for Boards
Read each in an hour • Quantity discounts up to 50 percent

The Ultimate Board Member's Book
Kay Sprinkel Grace, 114 pp., $24.95, ISBN 1889102180

Here is a book for *all* nonprofit boards: those wanting to operate with maximum effectiveness, those needing to clarify exactly what their job is, and those wanting to ensure that all members are 'on the same page.' It's all here in jargon-free language: how boards work, what the job entails, the time commitment, fundraising responsibilities, and much more.

How Are We Doing?
Gayle L. Gifford, 120 pp., $24.95, ISBN 1889102237

Until now, almost all books dealing with board evaluation have had an air of unreality about them. The perplexing graphs, the matrix boxes, the overlong questionnaires. Enter Gayle Gifford, who has pioneered an elegantly simple way for your board to evaluate and improve its overall performance. It all comes down to answering a host of simple, straightforward questions.

The Fundraising Habits of Supremely Successful Boards
Jerold Panas, 108 pp., $24.95, ISBN 1889102261

Jerold Panas has observed more boards at work than perhaps anyone in America, all the while helping them to surpass their campaign goals of $100,000 to $100 million. *Fundraising Habits* is the brilliant culmination of what Panas has learned firsthand about boards who excel at the task of resource development.

Big Gifts for Small Groups
Andy Robinson, 104 pp., $24.95, ISBN 1889102210

If yours is among the tens of thousands of organizations for whom six- and seven-figure gifts are unattainable, then this book is for you and your board. You'll learn everything you need to know: how to get ready for the campaign, whom to approach, where to find them, where to conduct the solicitation, what to bring with you, how to ask, how to make it easy for the donor to give, and what to do once you have the commitment.

Fundraising Mistakes that Bedevil All Boards (and Staff Too)
Kay Sprinkel Grace, 109 pp., $24.95, ISBN 1889102229

Fundraising mistakes are a thing of the past. Or, rather, there's no excuse for making a mistake anymore. If you blunder from now on, it's simply evidence you haven't read Kay Sprinkel Grace's book, in which she exposes *all* of the costly errors – 40 in total – that thwart us time and again.

Emerson & Church, Publishers
www.emersonandchurch.com

Copies of this and other books from the
publisher are available at discount when
purchased in quantity for boards of directors
or staff. Call 508-359-0019 or visit
www.emersonandchurch.com